The Prentice Hall Complete Book of

MODEL LETTERS, MEMOS and FORMS

for Secretaries

MARY A. DE VRIES

PRENTICE HALL
Englewood Cliffs, New Jersey 07632

Prentice-Hall International (UK) Limited, *London*
Prentice-Hall of Australia Pty. Limited, *Sydney*
Prentice-Hall Canada, Inc., *Toronto*
Prentice-Hall Hispanoamericana, S.A., *Mexico*
Prentice-Hall of India Private Limited, *New Delhi*
Prentice-Hall of Japan, Inc., *Tokyo*
Simon & Schuster Asia Pte. Ltd., *Singapore*
Editora Prentice-Hall do Brasil, Ltda., *Rio de Janeiro*

©1993 *by*
PRENTICE-HALL, Inc.
Englewood Cliffs, NJ

10 9 8 7 6 5 4 3 2 1

Library of Congress Cataloging-in-Publication Data

De Vries, Mary Ann.
    The Prentice Hall complete book of model letters, memos,
and forms for secretaries / Mary A. De Vries.
        p.   cm.
    Includes index.
    ISBN 0-13-720582-1 : $29.95
    1. Commercial correspondence—Handbooks, manuals, etc.
2. Memorandums—Handbooks, manuals, etc. 3. Letter-writing—
Handbooks, manuals, etc. 4. English language—Business
English—Handbooks, manuals, etc. I. Prentice-Hall, inc.
II. Title. III. Title: Complete book of model letters, memos,
and forms for secretaries.
HF5726.D479 1993   92-43928
651.7'4—dc20   CIP

ISBN 0-13-720582-1

PRENTICE HALL
Career & Personal Development
Englewood Cliffs, NJ 07632

Simon & Schuster, A Paramount Communications Company

Printed in the United States of America

About the Author

MARY A. DE VRIES has served as an editorial and communications consultant and has taught writing to many individual and organizational clients. She has had more than thirty professional and reference books published, including the *New American Handbook of Letter Writing*, *Guide to Better Business Writing*, *Prentice Hall Style Manual*, and *Complete Secretary's Handbook*.

Also by the Author

How to Use This Book

ALTHOUGH we live in an age of high-tech, high-speed messaging, computers and other forms of advanced technology haven't lessened the need to compose and send effective messages. Current technology has simply made it possible for us to create, process, and store more messages in less time with less drudgery. As the pressure for better and faster communication mounts, secretaries must rely more and more on good models to speed and improve their written communication. The model letters, memos, forms, and other types of communication provided in this book were designed to meet this need and can be adapted to electronic processing (electronic mail, facsimile, telex, and so on) as well as conventional letter writing.

Although model messages were useful timesavers before electronic typewriters and computers became commonplace, the benefits are even greater now since formats, stock phrases, and even entire messages can be stored electronically for later recall and editing to suit some future communication need. The specific details may change in each message, and condensed versions of a long conventional letter may be needed for electronic mail, telex, and certain other forms of fast messaging, but other aspects of letter writing remain the same. The basic letter or memo format and the tone, general approach or pattern, and opening and closing will very often be the same in most types of correspondence. Thus a basic message can be used over and over except for changing names, dates, and figures.

Each time you prepare a message that fits a relatively standard pattern, such as a letter of recommendation or a memo reminding someone of a deadline, store it in your computer forms file and print out a copy for your notebook or file folder of hard-copy models. You can add the models in this book to your computer file one at a time, as you use each one, or if your office has a scanner, you can transfer the entire collection all at once, incorporating the various categories of the book into your own index of models. (The Model Selector Guide on pages xxv–lvii may serve as a basis for your index.)

The 400 models in this book, including the 70 model forms in chapters 17 and 18, were prepared on a personal computer. Included are models of letters, memos, announcements, invitations, forms, and key parts of reports and press releases. These models are grouped in four parts, followed by a fifth part in which the principal elements of a message, including envelopes, mailing labels, and business cards, are discussed.

Part I: Letters

Part II: Memos

Part III: Other Messages

Part IV: Forms

Part V: Letter-Writing Aids

Part I has twelve chapters of model letters covering the major areas of professional and business communication. Although practices vary from office to office in regard to who signs a particular letter, the models provided here can be adjusted to suit the preferred practice in your office.

1. Requests and Inquiries

2. Reservations and Orders

3. Acknowledgments

4. Reminders and Follow-Ups

5. Appointments

6. Introductions and Recommendations

7. Employees

8. Appreciation and Goodwill

9. Social-Business Messages

10. Complaints and Adjustments

11. Credit and Collection

12. Sales Promotion

Part II has two chapters of model memos illustrating the two principal types of internal and external memos. The format used for both types of memos is the same and is also the preferred format in electronic mail and other computer-based message systems.

13. Memos That Give Information

14. Memos That Make a Request

Part III has two chapters of other communication models, including formal social-business messages (chapter 15) and models of informational business reporting (chapter 16).

15. Announcements and Invitations

16. Reports and Press Releases

Part IV has two chapters of timesaving model forms grouped in two key categories:

17. Communication Forms

18. Record-Keeping Forms

Part V has two chapters of letter-writing aids that illustrate each physical part of a message and explain how to position the various elements on a page.

19. Letter and Memo Formats

20. Principal Elements of Letters and Memos

Since a principal objective of a letter book is to help you save time in preparing your correspondence, the ease with which you can locate the models you need is an important consideration. In this book, the Contents and the Model Selector Guide offer you two options in locating models for use.

The Model Selector Guide is an alphabetical subject index to the models, and the Contents identifies the principal categories of models in each chapter and the specific models within each category. In chapter 8, "Appreciation and Goodwill," for example, sixteen models concern messages of appreciation (8.1–8.16), seven involve various goodwill letters (8.17–8.23), and nine focus on the special category of congratulatory messages (8.24–8.32). Models are numbered consecutively within each chapter, beginning each time with the number 1 (8.1, 9.1, 10.1, and so on).

Assume that you need to write a letter to a company complaining about its poor service and, particularly, its late deliveries. If you scan the Contents, you will see numerous models about complaints in chapter 10. According to the Contents, the third model in the chapter, listed as follows, appears on page 122.

--- **10** ---

Complaints and Adjustments

❖ Making Complaints
  ◆ Incomplete Shipment
    10.1 Of Stationery
  ◆ Unsatisfactory Performance: Individual
    10.2 Of Employee
  ◆ Unsatisfactory Service: Company
    10.3 Late Deliveries

If you turn to the appropriate page for model 10.3, you will find a letter complaining about a company's consistently late deliveries on orders. The writer of this model not only registers a complaint but tells the company that it must correct the situation or the buyer will be forced to find a new supplier.

The Model Selector Guide, located at the front of the book after the Contents, provides a thorough, easy-to-use index for locating models quickly. There you can find almost any subject listed alphabetically, with the associated model numbers beside it. Consider again the problem about poor service, particularly late deliveries. You have two key words in this example: *service* and *deliveries*. If you look in the *D* section of the Model Selector Guide for "Deliveries," you will see this listing:

❖ Deliveries
- complaints about 10.3
- confirming details 2.6, 2.11-2.12
- delays 2.9, 3.13, 10.17, 10.20
- incomplete 10.1, 10.18
- inquiries about 1.2, 1.8, 14.23
- instructions 2.4, 4.15

Notice that the first topic is "complaints about" deliveries, and the model for this topic is number 10.3.

If you look in the *S* section of the Model Selector Guide for "Service," you will find this listing:

❖ Service
- changing order for 2.8, 13.22
- on committee 3.9, 9.9
- complaints about 10.3, 10.19
- to former customers 12.12
- inquiries about 14.23
- introducing 6.5, 12.1
- ordering 2.5
- requesting information about 1.1

In this case the third category is "complaints about" service, and two models (10.3 and 10.19) are mentioned.

Since the Model Selector Guide includes all major topics in the book listed alphabetically for convenience, it should immediately point to the models you want to see.

To form a database for this book, hundreds of organizations from all parts of the United States provided sample correspondence and other material for evaluation: businesses such as manufacturing, retail, and wholesale establishments; service organizations such as travel agencies, printers, advertising agencies, and consulting firms; nonprofit organizations such as colleges, professional societies, secretarial schools, research institutions, and churches; and publishing and communications firms such as magazine and book publishers and television stations. Thousands of messages were collected from every conceivable source, touching upon activities as diverse as jewelry repair, the sale of insurance, long-distance moving, and computer programming. All of these messages were evaluated, categorized, and distilled to form the 400 models selected for inclusion in this book.

Mary A. De Vries

Contents

——————————— *Part I* ———————————

LETTERS 1

——————————— **1** ———————————

Requests and Inquiries 3

2

Reservations and Orders 19

3

Acknowledgment Letters 29

4

Reminders and Follow-ups 39

5

Appointment Letters 49

6

Introductions and Recommendations 57

7

Employees 71

8

Appreciation and Goodwill 87

9

Social-Business Messages 105

10

Complaints and Adjustments 119

11

Credit and Collection 135

12

Sales Promotion 149

Part II

MEMOS 163

13

Memos That Give Information 165

14

Memos That Make a Request 191

—————————— *Part III* ——————————

OTHER MESSAGES 211

—————————————— **15** ——————————————

Announcements and Invitations 213

16

Reports and Press Releases   221

Part IV

FORMS 239

17

Communications Forms 241

18

Record-Keeping Forms 261

Part V

LETTER-WRITING AIDS 315

19

Letter and Memo Formats 317

—————————————— **20** ——————————————

Principal Elements of Letters and Memos 333

Model Selector Guide

Part

I

LETTERS

1

Requests and Inquiries

REQUESTS and inquiries are two of the most common types of letters to come into and go out of an office. In fact, they sometimes make up the lion's share of a secretary's daily correspondence. It is obvious, then, why these letters must be handled quickly and efficiently. In a modern office a busy secretary has no time to waste needlessly on repetitive, routine tasks. The model letters in this chapter are intended to save you precious time each day as you process requests and inquiries. Store the letters in your computer where they can be recalled and edited to fit each new situation. (The Model Selector Guide will direct you to other letters pertaining to requests and inquiries such as "Responding to Requests for Appointments" in chapter 5.)

Depending on the practice in your office, you will probably write many of these letters for your own signature (such as 1.1.); you may also write some of them for your boss's signature (such as 1.19); and your boss may draft others and ask you to refine and polish them (such as 1.14). Add these new letters to your computer file. If you have any doubts about who should respond to a particular letter, ask your boss what he or she prefers. The nice thing about requests and inquiries is that they usually fall into a pattern that soon becomes easy to recognize.

Inquiries may be general (asking for information about new software) or specific (asking about prices and availability of printer ribbons). Many inquiries also include a request. Replies to inquiries fall into more categories (such as answering a specific question, offering more than the writer requests, or enclosing literature with the response). Letters 1.1 through 1.7 are examples of typical letters of inquiry and replies to inquiries. (See chapter 14 for examples of inquiries transmitted by memo.)

Some letters of request, although similar in many ways to a routine inquiry letter, often require more thought. A request for a raise (see 1.10), for instance, necessitates great care in preparation; it must present a forceful, persuasive case for the writer. Similarly, responses to requests can be sensitive. Perhaps the answer must be negative, such as saying no to someone. Nevertheless it must be done without offending the person. Letters 1.8 through 1.20 are examples of typical letters of request and responses to requests. (See also chapter 14 for requests made by memo.)

MAKING INQUIRIES

An inquiry must be straightforward and specific, and *all* letters should be courteous and considerate. Keep the inquiry as brief as possible.

1. Explain why you are writing, if pertinent.
2. State specifically what information you want.
3. Indicate if you want the reader to take some action.

The following two models say just enough—but not too much—for the reader to be able to decide quickly what to do and how to reply.

General Inquiry

1.1. About Service

Ladies and Gentlemen:

We have heard about your new nationwide custom-processing service for photographers. Is this service available in Memphis? If not, please send us the address of the nearest lab. Thank you.

Sincerely,

Authorities disagree on the use of "thank you" to conclude a letter, particularly a routine inquiry like model 1.1. Most writers and readers, however, consider any brief statement of appreciation to be a mark of courtesy and any omission of one to be a mark of rudeness. Some offices follow the practice of concluding a letter addressed to a specific person with the friendlier, more casual phrase, "Thanks very much."

Inquiry for Specific Needs

1.2. About Delivery Date

Dear Mr. Harmon:

Would it be possible to receive the fourteen 8 x 10 glossy prints I ordered on May 24 one week earlier than requested? Our photography workshop has been rescheduled for an earlier date, and we'll need the prints by June 12 at the latest. Would it help if I picked them up at your studio to save mail time?

I'd appreciate anything you can do to meet this new deadline. Please telephone me at 616-7777 to confirm that the prints will be available by June 12; also, please let me know if I should plan to pick them up.

Thanks very much.

Sincerely,

Specific inquiries must provide specific information; if Mr. Harmon's photography studio had been larger or if the writer had worked in a larger office, the inquiry might also have included a purchase order number and other pertinent reference data.

RESPONDING TO INQUIRIES

Since many inquiries come from potential customers, a prompt reply can contribute to an eventual sale. At the very least, a quick response can help build goodwill for your company.

1. Provide as much information as you can in your first sentence.
2. Give specific information.
3. If further communication or action is needed or is desirable, make a recommendation.
4. Thank the writer for his or her interest.

Models 1.3 through 1.7 provide typical replies to five common types of inquiries.

Response to Specific Questions

1.3. On Procedure

Dear Mr. Sims:

It was good to hear that you would like to display your cookware at our fair. Space is being reserved now for such exhibits, and I suggest you make your decision about taking a booth by August 20.

The enclosed literature will describe the physical attributes of the exhibit area, and the entry form contains information on fees and hours during which exhibits will be open to the public. All you need to do to reserve a booth is to complete the entry form and mail it with your check to this office. Details on setting up your exhibit will be sent promptly upon receipt of your reservation.

I hope the enclosed material will answer your questions, but do let me know if I can add anything. Thanks very much for telling us about your cookware. I'll look forward to seeing your exhibit at the fair.

Sincerely,

Even when you use an occasion such as this to do some selling on the side, your first objective must be to answer the writer's questions clearly and thoughtfully.

Reply That Offers Additional Information

1.4. About Order

Dear Ms. Hendricks:

Yes, the discount on 35mm cameras you inquired about is still available and does apply to the models you saw listed in our catalog. Through December 15 all brands will be sold at 25 percent off our regularly listed prices, and you may, indeed, order by mail.

The cameras are being offered at a discount in addition to our usual low prices. They are current models we are clearing out to make room for a supply of new models arriving in January. (The new models, however, will not be available at these discount prices.) Just pick any camera shown in this year's catalog and deduct 25 percent from the listed price. As the catalog order form shows, we pay postage and handling on all mail orders over $10.

If we can provide more information to help you make a selection, please let us know. We appreciate your interest in our cameras.

Sincerely,

This letter does some soft selling, but it first answers the writer's question—whether the discount is still available. Since Ms. Hendricks appeared to be interested in knowing as much as possible, the response also tells *why* the cameras are being discounted.

Reply When the Inquiry Is Vague

1.5. About Statistical Information

Dear Mr. Collins:

We were pleased to learn that your article on successful merchandising techniques for your school newspaper will use our company as an example. Two booklets that describe our company's operations and products are enclosed.

I'll also be glad to send some statistical information as you requested. Please let me know what kind of statistical data you need: company figures, such as number of employees and plants, or product figures, such as products manufactured and shipped? Also, since our statistical information is so extensive, covering more than twenty years of operations, I'll need to know what years are of interest to you and whether you want various breakdowns of statistics, such as products shipped nationally or by region, state, or city. If you are uncertain about what you need at this early stage, perhaps you could describe your proposed article in detail, and I could then select figures that I believe would be most useful to you.

Best of luck in your research. We're happy to be of help and appreciate your thinking of our company.

Cordially,

This letter depicts a typical situation. When inquiries are vague, the best thing to do is ask the writer to be more specific. Take care, however, not to let any sign of annoyance creep into your letter. As a representative of your company you must be courteous and helpful at all times.

Reply When Information Is Not Available

1.6. About Product

Dear Ms. Jones:

We wholeheartedly agree that our vitamins and cosmetics should be made available over the counter in stores throughout the country--and we're working on that right now! Although it's a little too early to specify when this will occur or in which stores the products will be sold, we hope to have this information available by June.

The announcement of sales through retail outlets--large department stores, chain drug stores, and so on--will be made in our monthly catalog, probably in the May issue. Since you're on our mailing list, you'll be receiving the announcement in this way. Although we hope a store near you will carry our products, everything will continue to be available by mail, and you will receive a new catalog each month, just as before.

It's good to know you value our vitamins and cosmetics so highly. You may be certain we value your trust in us just as highly. Thanks for letting us know about your interest in the retail distribution of our products.

Sincerely,

Letter 1.6 illustrates another frequent situation—the need to say *something* that will satisfy the writer, even though the information specifically requested is not available. In these cases, avoid a negative reply such as "I don't know; write back later."

Transmittal Letter

1.7. About Prices, with Form to Be Completed

Dear Mr. Tryon:

Here is the current price list you requested. You'll notice that it covers our full line of automobile parts and accessories.

An order form appears at the bottom of the price list. To order the items you need, simply check them off in the spaces provided, complete the form, and return it to us.

Thanks for your interest. I hope we hear from you again.

Sincerely,

Transmittal letters are sometimes prepared as printed "Dear Customer" form letters or are printed with only the inside address and salutation filled in each time. If the items transmitted are few, however, or if they continually differ (such as a report, a brochure, a price list, or a sample of something), each transmittal letter may be prepared individually or a computer model edited to suit each situation. Model 1.7 could be used either as a printed form letter or as an individually prepared letter.

MAKING REQUESTS

The inquiry often does no more than ask about something (What do your computer tables cost?), but the request always asks to have something done (Send us two computer tables). Like the inquiry, the request must be specific.

1. Tell what you want (possibly why you want it).
2. Explain what action you want the reader to take.
3. Specify all pertinent facts, such as time, place, price, delivery.
4. Express appreciation if a favor or special effort is required.

Models 1.8 through 1.12 are examples of five common types of requests.

Request Without Alternative

1.8. For Action

Dear Janice:

Would it be possible for you to have the electronic display boards we ordered yesterday ready a few days before our Monday afternoon marketing meeting? I will be helping Mr. Dexter finish his presentation materials over the weekend; if the boards were already set up we could test how well the display items work on the boards at the same time. We're a little worried about one display and would feel much safer if we could check it out before Monday.

Please telephone me at 666-1212 if you can have the boards here by Friday noon on June 5. Incidentally, I'll be glad to help you set them up. Thanks so much for your help, Janice.

Best wishes,

Although model 1.10 is called the "Persuasive Request," all requests are persuasive to some degree, as you can see from model 1.8. Often the "why" of the request is very important and should be mentioned early in the letter; however, all that is needed is just enough to persuade the reader to say yes—not pages and pages of facts that are of no use or interest to the reader. Notice in this model that the writer uses the recipient's name in concluding: "Thanks so much for your help, Janice." Experience shows that this is an effective letter-writing technique and can be used frequently to good advantage.

Request with Alternative

1.9. For a Decision

Dear Joe:

How would you feel about taking action to end the growing controversy over our proposed clubhouse? As treasurer of the Lakeville
Country Club Association, you might be able to settle things once
and for all.

The principal disagreement among members is over the size of the
proposed clubhouse expenditure. Some people think the commitment of funds would be unrealistic for us. There's only one way to
find out: get three bids from reputable contractors and have both
the bids and our financial status examined in depth. Specifically,
you could propose to the membership that we retain a local accounting firm to undertake this examination and submit recommendations to us. The other alternative would be for you to make the
study; however, I realize that it would be extremely difficult for you
to make a commitment to donate that much time and effort to
such a project. Also, if the study came from the outside, no one
could claim bias in the recommendations. Would you therefore
want to get a quote from a local accounting firm?

Please let me know your decision as soon as possible, Joe. I would
agree to either course of action, just so we do something to settle
the debate before the controversy becomes even more heated.

Best regards,

When more than one alternative is given in a letter, the writer
should ask certain questions before stating the alternatives. For
example, are they of equal merit? Are all equally practical and
desirable? Would the choice of a particular alternative create special
problems that should be mentioned? In model 1.9 the writer obviously
prefers one of the two alternatives but is eager to do *something*
and thus would agree to either of them.

Persuasive Request

1.10. For a Raise

Dear Dr. Carlton:

Today I'm starting my third year of employment at Raleigh Junior
College and my second year in your office. I've enjoyed every moment and hope the progress we've all shared has been satisfying
to you too. I'd appreciate it very much if you would review my ac-

complishments during the past two years and consider a salary increase for me effective the first of next month.

Since I've worked in your office, our secretarial and clerical staff has grown from one person to four, including part-time student assistants. As a result, my responsibilities have increased greatly, primarily in the areas of training and supervising assistants. To handle the growing work load that made this staff expansion necessary, I've made a number of significant contributions: For example, I established a new electronic filing system, streamlined the mail-processing function, developed a more effective computerized follow-up system for our counseling activities, and prepared a work manual for all of us to use as a guide to office practices and procedures. In addition to making these specific contributions, I believe that my word processing skills have improved substantially during the past two years and that I am performing all of my duties more confidently and more effectively each day.

I hope the above examples of progress are evident in my record of performance at Raleigh and that you'll agree they justify an increase in my salary.

Thank you very much, Dr. Carlton, for considering my request.

Sincerely,

A persuasive request is really a selling job, which means that you have to state in your letter as many good reasons as you can think of to support your case. Such a letter requires careful planning. You should list and refine all of the reasons you want to use before you begin composing the letter. Once you start writing, present your case in logical order. Guard against unreasonable requests and inaccurate statements.

Personal Request

1.11. For a Favor

Dear Jeff:

Could you spare about thirty minutes of your time next Friday at 2:30 p.m. to meet a friend of mine, Will Blackwell?

Will has joined our firm as assistant production manager, and I'd like to help him feel at home in our firm. I'd appreciate it if you could spend a little time with him to become acquainted and to introduce him to your department's activities. The better he knows his way around all of our departments, the sooner he will feel comfortable in his new position.

If you can fit this into your busy schedule, Jeff, please call me at 301-9343. Many thanks.

Best regards,

Requesting a favor may involve imposing on someone else, so it is important to let the person know *why* you are asking, to make the request as reasonable as possible, and always to show your appreciation. When appropriate, it also never hurts to offer something in return.

Fund-Raising Request

1.12. For School Library

Dear Mrs. Slocumbe:

As a graduate of Fulton Junior College, no one knows better than you the importance of up-to-date library facilities and resources. With the help of many generous alumni such as you, we have expanded our collections and services each year during the past decade. But the cost of maintaining adequate facilities has increased so dramatically in recent years that, for the first time, we may be unable to add to our collections or even to maintain the overall standards of past years.

We are particularly concerned about the limited number of computer stations that we can offer the students, with the result that long lines form each day at each terminal, and many students return to class with incomplete assignments. Therefore, we are asking our supporters to provide a 10 percent or greater increase over their gifts of last year. Our students join us in asking you to help us help them.

Large or small, however, your gift this year will bring us closer to our goal of providing the best services and facilities possible for our expanding enrollment. Please send your contribution today in the enclosed envelope.

Sincerely,

Fund-raising letters, as model 1.12 illustrates, typically explain—persuasively—why more money is needed and then appeal to the givers' pride or satisfaction in helping. Usually, these letters are standard form letters, although each one may carry the recipient's inside address and name to give it a personal appearance.

RESPONDING TO REQUESTS

The request, like the routine inquiry, often comes from a prospective customer, and promptness and courtesy in replying are essential.

1. Be specific and clear in your response.
2. If you must say no or maybe, be considerate.
3. Recommend further action or communication, if necessary.

Models 1.11 through 1.20 are examples of ten typical situations requiring a variety of responses to requests.

Reply That Offers More than Requested

1.13. For Clarification

Dear Lynn:

We'd be glad to send you an address list of our society's membership on press-apply labels. However, the price of $65 a thousand that I had quoted was for a standard printout; the charge for a printout on press-apply labels is $95 a thousand. Shall we go ahead on that basis? Please let me know--thanks, Lynn.

Best wishes,

When you suspect that a person making a request has misunderstood something or lacks important information, *do not* proceed until you have sent a clarification.

Granting a Request for a Future Date

1.14. For Interview

Dear Ms. Pace:

Thank you for sending us your resume. We do have an opening in the File Department, and Mr. Johnson would be happy to discuss the position with you.

Could you come in on Thursday morning, November 5? Mr. Johnson will be free at 10:30 a.m. Please telephone me at 625-9999 if you are unable to come at that time. Otherwise, we'll look forward to seeing you then.

Cordially,

Although some letters, such as model 1.14, should be brief, they need not be abrupt. Notice how the last sentence of this letter adds a friendly, warm tone; in this case, it may also help to relax a nervous job applicant.

Positive Response That Suggests Alternative

1.15. To Assistance

Dear Ms. Marshall:

I was pleased to learn that you would like to have someone from our office assist you in organizing a local chapter of our state's Human Resources Council. Naturally, I'm flattered that you thought of me, and it is with regret that I must decline the opportunity to work with you on this project. My unpredictable schedule just wouldn't allow me to do justice to the effort.

Have you considered my assistant Hal Goldman? He's a super-organizer and seems to have boundless energy and enthusiasm once he gets involved in a project. Also, he has lived in this community most of his adult life and knows where to go and whom to see for support and cooperation in local activities. Since part of his job is to keep our office functioning smoothly while I'm traveling, he would be available most of the time. I know Hal enjoys this type of project work, and I'm certain you could count on a positive response from him.

Although I'm sorry that I can't personally participate, it would be satisfying to me to know that someone from our office was involved in this important venture. Many thanks for asking, and please accept my good wishes for a successful Human Resources chapter.

Cordially,

Model 1.15 illustrates a common situation—agreeing to a general idea but suggesting an alternative to the writer's specific request. A reply of this type should move rapidly into a persuasive case for the alternative suggestion, so the emphasis of the letter and its tone will be positive and will not discourage the person making the request.

Transmittal Letter

1.16. For Literature, with Documents Enclosed

Dear Mr. Cramer:

Here, with our compliments, are the three reports you requested: "Wastewater Treatment"; "The Sloan Watershed Project"; and "Changing Rural Land-Use Patterns."

I hope this literature will be helpful to you. Thanks very much for writing to the Science Institute.

Sincerely,

Transmittal letters are usually brief, the intent being simply to say that certain items are enclosed (or are being sent separately). However, there is no reason why a transmittal letter has to be cold and unfriendly, as you can see from the last paragraph of model 1.16.

Authorization Letter

1.17. For Report

Dear Ms. Pacheco:

This will authorize you to prepare a report for Benjamin K. Arquette, president, Keystone Toys, Inc. A copy of the request from Mr. Arquette is enclosed, and it explains the scope and type of information desired.

Please focus primarily on ways that Keystone executives can more effectively budget and control their time, including basic steps in mastering time priorities, scheduling strategies, and timesaving management techniques. Also, please keep in mind that because of the changing nature of Keystone's product, the executives are continually adjusting their work loads to accommodate new projects. This factor, therefore, should be built into your analysis.

I'll look forward to reviewing a draft of your report on or before June 7. In the meantime, please let me know if you have any questions concerning this authorization or the report itself.

Sincerely,

Report authorizations are letters and memos that tell someone to prepare a report, summarize the content and scope required, and specify a deadline. They may be directed to a preparer within the firm or to someone in an outside firm that specializes in research and report preparation.

Unqualified Refusal

1.18. For Contribution

Dear Mr. Moore:

I regret very much that our company will be unable to contribute to your drive to secure recreational funds for underprivileged children in our community. As much as we would like to support all such worthwhile endeavors, our company is small, and we are forced to confine our donations to a single annual pledge to the Community Fund.

Please accept our good wishes for the success of your campaign for this important cause.

Sincerely,

A letter of refusal should include a reason for declining the request. Model 1.18 concerns a worthy cause and thus the letter closes with good wishes for the project's success.

Qualified Refusal

1.19. Of Cooperation

Dear Paula:

Thanks for giving me a chance to review your proposal for a new system to handle registrations at our next seminar. You obviously spent a lot of time on this. Although I agree that the chaos we experienced at last year's seminar must be prevented in the future, I'm reluctant to recommend this new system to Mr. Parks.

The greatest difficulty I anticipate in the proposed system is the need to have the registration desk run by two persons from our secretarial staff instead of volunteers from the seminar. Although that might prevent chaos at the registration desk, I'm afraid it would introduce chaos in our office. We usually have a peak work load at the time of our seminars and really need more, not less, help.

I know you would like to solve the problem, and so would I. But perhaps we need to move in a different direction--such as computerization of this activity--and find a solution that won't affect our work capacity and capability at the office. If you can come up with an idea that avoids such pitfalls, let me know, and I'll be delighted to help you put it into effect.

Thanks for all your time and effort, Paula. I know everyone on the training committee will appreciate it.

Best wishes,

The qualified refusal is tricky to write, as model 1.19 suggests. Often the objective is to say "No, I won't unless . . ." Like any kind of refusal, this one requires tact and consideration for the feelings of the recipient.

Referral to Other Sources

1.20. For Additional Information

Dear Mr. Inman:

Since our department no longer conducts market research, the information we have on machine tool orders and shipments is both limited and dated. Have you contacted the Machine Control magazine in Dayton? It has a very active research department and might be able to supply the figures you need. Also, you might write to the Department of Commerce's Metalworking Division for back issues of its quarterly industrial reports.

Good luck in finding the information you need, and thanks for thinking of us.

Sincerely,

It is always a matter of good public relations to be as helpful as possible to anyone who contacts you. This includes taking time to compose a pleasant, even if brief, letter pointing out a better source to the writer.

2

Reservations and Orders

ACCURACY is a principal consideration in preparing and processing reservations and orders. Thus when information is secured or conveyed by telephone, it is usually confirmed by letter.

Although purchase order or requisition forms (see "Orders" in chapter 18) are commonly used to place orders, letters or memos (see "Processing Orders" in chapter 13) may also be used. The models in chapter 2 illustrate the use of letters to process reservations and orders.

You may write and sign a majority of these letters (such as 2.1) but will draft other letters (such as 2.9) for your boss's signature. Regardless of the practice in your office, the sample letters in this chapter can easily be adapted to your situation; just follow the general pattern of the letters using your own information in each case. If you keep model reservation letters and orders in a computer file, they can be copied for editing on screen. Models 2.1 through 2.3 are examples of messages pertaining to reservations. (See chapter 3 for models of orders acknowledged by letter.)

Although travel reservations are usually requested by telephone and handled by a company travel department or an outside travel agency, certain reservations may be made by letter. Examples of such letters are those requesting information (2.1) or confirming reservations (2.2).

Placing orders is a common task in most offices even when a company purchasing department exists. Although forms may be used to place most orders, a letter may be required to deal with related matters such as delays (2.9), information requests (2.10), and confirmations (2.11). Models 2.4 through 2.12 are examples of letters concerning the placement or receipt of orders.

HANDLING RESERVATIONS

Reservation letters are usually brief, but they must give all necessary facts to avoid mistakes that could create problems later.

1. Be absolutely clear and specific in transmitting both requests and acknowledgments.
2. Give all pertinent facts, for example, times, places, dates, order numbers, and check or credit numbers.
3. Ask for (and give) written confirmations when appropriate.

Models 2.1 to 2.3 are typical reservation letters that a secretary usually writes.

Requesting Information on Availability, Rates

2.1. For Hotel Accommodations

Ladies and Gentlemen:

Please send your rates for a single room with bath, fourth floor or lower. Would you have something available from Monday afternoon, March 4, through the night of Wednesday, March 6?

I'd appreciate an immediate reply so that I can make reservations right away. Thank you.

Sincerely,

Inquiries such as model 2.1 can be very brief, containing only the essential facts. It is not necessary at this point to give the name of the person for whom a reservation will eventually be made. (If time is short, this type of inquiry could be made by facsimile or telephone.)

Confirming Reservation

2.2. For Dinner

Dear Mr. Thomas:

This will confirm your reservation for a dinner table for twelve on Tuesday, March 4, at 7:30 p.m. in our Sunflower Room.

We will be happy to provide the full-course roast beef menu you selected, with the services of a wine steward, at $15.95 per person.

If there is anything additional we can do to make the evening enjoyable for you and your guests, please do let me know. We appreciate the opportunity to help you plan this special occasion.

Sincerely,

Reservation confirmations can be brief, summarizing only the essential facts. But if you are providing a service and hope to have the customer return again, it is important to add a word of appreciation or a thoughtful offer of further assistance (such as the last paragraph of model 2.2).

Pickup-Delivery Arrangements

2.3. For Theater Tickets

Ladies and Gentlemen:

Please reserve two mezzanine seats for the November 14 evening performance of "The Window Dresser." Fred Beal, our company representative, will pick up the tickets at the box office on the afternoon of November 14.

A check for $88 is enclosed. Please let us know which seats are being reserved and confirm that the two tickets will be available at the box office for Mr. Beal on November 14. A stamped, self-addressed envelope is enclosed for your convenience in replying.

Thank you.

Sincerely,

When a ticket agency is unavailable or when a written copy of a request is required for the files, a letter is used to make the reservation. The tickets themselves can be mailed, delivered by messenger, or held for pickup. Whichever method you choose, make clear in your letter the date desired for delivery or pickup.

PROCESSING ORDERS

When the need for personal handling precludes the use of a standard order or acknowledgment form, orders must be processed by letter.

1. Specify clearly what you want to order. In an acknowledgment, confirm exactly what has been ordered.

2. Make certain that all facts are correct and clearly understood regarding things such as price, quantity, and delivery date.

3. If any changes are necessary, carefully explain what is required.

4. Thank the customer for the order.

Models 2.4 to 2.12 are examples of the variety of orders that are processed by letter.

Placing Order: Payment by Credit Card

2.4. For Merchandise

Ladies and Gentlemen:

Please send us the following item from your office furnishings department:

One (1), catalog no. R-497560, 6 x 9, Oatmeal, Fiber Blend Area Rug by RugMakers Ltd., $399.98 plus tax.

The purchase should be charged to the Statewide account of Martin West, senior vice president, West Enterprises (account number 6621-0044-3976), and it should be delivered to West Enterprises, Suite 211, 1006 Highway North, Falls Church, VA 22042, attention Brenda Short.

I'd appreciate written acknowledgment of this order, along with your estimated delivery date for the rug. Thank you.

Sincerely,

To avoid confusion, the delivery address should also specify the name of the individual who will receive the item or sign for it.

Placing Order: Payment by Check

2.5. For Service

Dear Ms. Jennings:

Thanks very much for explaining the procedure to initiate business telephone service for Cole Records Company in our new Midwest office.

We would like to have service established effective April 6 in Room 112, 23-14 Lafayette Avenue, Des Moines, IA 50336. One of our pany representatives will be there from 9 to 5 o'clock on April 6 to indicate the precise location of telephone jacks to be activated.

Enclosed is our company check 2358 for $97.50, which includes a $55.00 deposit and $42.50 installation fee. Monthly bills and should be sent to our eastern office: Cole Records Company, Inc., 511 West 42nd Street, New York, NY 10017.

Thanks for all your help, Ms. Jennings. Please let me know if you need any further information. In the meantime, I'd appreciate your confirmation of this order.

Cordially,

Requests for telephone service and similar orders can usually be made by telephone, but a letter is often desired to provide a file copy of the request and to provide remittance advice. If a deposit is required for the service or product you are ordering, state the amount in your letter and what it covers so that the recipient will know if you have misunderstood any instructions.

Confirmation of Telephone Order

2.6. *For Office Equipment*

Dear Mr. Ryan:

Thank you for your August 9 telephone order for one (1) model 320 camel-colored, high-back vinyl side chair, at our sale price of $249.98 plus $22.00 shipping and handling. The chair will be shipped from our factory in North Carolina in about four weeks; it will be sent to you C.O.D. as you requested.

We appreciate your order very much and hope we can be of service again.

Sincerely,

It is especially important to confirm a telephone order, and computer-generated letters or forms are common for this purpose. Whether sent by letter or on a confirmation form, the acknowledgment must restate all facts—full description, price and other charges, delivery date, and so on—to avoid any misunderstandings later. Details of telephone conversations may soon be forgotten.

Canceling Order: Payment by Credit Card

2.7. For Literature

Ladies and Gentlemen:

On February 5 I placed an order for two correspondence courses: Basic Bookkeeping No. 343. The courses were charged to Ronald Page's First National Credit Card 4-606-2197-001.

Since the persons for whom this material was intended have been transferred to another division, we will be unable to use the courses. Please cancel the order and credit Mr. Page's account in full.

I'd appreciate having written confirmation of this cancellation. Thank you for your help.

Sincerely,

A cancellation of an order, like the original order, should state all pertinent data. If the order has already been received and can be returned, the letter should state that the unused material is enclosed for a full refund (if paid by check) or full credit (if charged to an account).

Changing Order: Payment by Check

2.8. For Maintenance

Dear Mr. Bloomington:

We would like to change our recent order for typewriter maintenance service at Benson Supplies, Inc. We had requested a maintenance contract for four of our electronic office machines, and a check for $480 for one year's coverage was sent to you on July 15.

One of the typewriters included in this agreement has since been sold, and we would like to change the contract to cover service for just the three remaining machines. In your June 4 letter to Barkley Briggs, associate director at Benson Supplies, you state that coverage for three machines would be $390. Please refund to Benson Supplies, Inc., the balance due ($90) as a result of this reduction in service.

I'm enclosing a copy of our present contract and will look forward to receiving a revised agreement. Thanks very much.

Sincerely,

Revised orders often involve refunds or additional charges. In the case of a refund, your letter must specify to whom a check should be sent or which account should be credited.

Apology for Delay

2.9. Of Parts

Dear Mr. Creighton:

I'm very sorry for the unavoidable delay we've encountered in shipping the parts to you for your press. The recent truckers' strike created an unexpected backlog of orders at our factory, and all shipments had to be rescheduled. Now that the transportation problem has been solved, we will be able to ship the parts by October 5. I hope this date will be satisfactory.

Please accept our sincere apologies for any inconvenience the delay has caused. We appreciate your patience.

Cordially,

The tone of a letter of apology is particularly important since the letter must try to alleviate the customer's annoyance. First, an apology should be extended, and then, a solution should be offered.

Need Additional Information to Fill Order

2.10. For Subscription

Dear Ms. Ritter:

Yes, we would be very happy to enter a subscription to Homebuilder's Newsletter for you and each of the other twenty-four members of your club and, as you requested, send an invoice for the full amount.

The group subscription rate is $16 per person for twelve issues or $24 per person for twenty-four issues. Please specify your choice on the enclosed invoice. As you can see, the two-year rate will offer a substantial savings ($200 savings for twenty-five subscriptions).

We will need one further item of information from you to complete our records: should all copies be sent to you each month, or will you be providing mailing addresses for the other twenty-four members? As soon as we hear from you we'll complete your subscription records, and the first issue will soon be on the way.

Thanks so much for your interest in <u>Homebuilders' Newsletter</u>. I hope you enjoy and profit from each fact-filled issue.

Cordially,

It's common for orders to come in with facts insufficient to fill them. If printed forms are not used for soliciting the required information, a letter must be sent. Since you are dealing with a customer or prospective customer, your letter must not show any irritation, even if the writer forgot something obvious; rather, it should be pleasant and indicate your appreciation for the customer's order.

Confirmation of Price-Delivery Time

2.11. For Supplies

Dear Mr. Jones:

This will confirm the offer regarding clipboards that I made to you by telephone yesterday. We can supply 400 gold-stamped, navy vinyl clipboards, 9 x 12, with ruled tablet inserts, for $598 plus 6 percent sales tax, to be delivered to your offices on or before March 23. So that we can meet your deadline, please let us know by February 15 whether you wish to have us proceed with the order.

If we can be of help in any other way, just let me know. Thanks very much for asking about our convention supplies.

Sincerely,

Confirmations of prices should clearly specify any extra charges such as shipping or sales tax. If you promise to deliver goods by a specific date, be certain to tell the prospective customer when he or she must place the order in order for you to meet that deadline.

Transmittal Letter

2.12. For Shipment

Dear Carl:

Fourteen insured cartons of files and other materials are being sent to you today by Hillyer Trucking Service. This will complete the transfer of records to our new office. As you know, I will personally hand-carry our bank books, books of account, and other vital records.

Hope everything arrives safely. I'll be joining you in a few weeks--in time to help you unpack!

Best regards,

Although we usually think of packing slips or special forms accompanying the shipment of materials, there are other occasions when a separate, individually prepared letter is needed or preferred. A copy of the transmittal letter is often enclosed in each carton of material.

3

Acknowledgment Letters

ACKNOWLEDGING correspondence is common courtesy in a business office. Although many routine acknowledgments are handled with a standard form, others require more personal attention. The models in chapter 3 are grouped into two basic categories of acknowledgments: those that acknowledge a letter without answering it and those that acknowledge and also answer it.

You will always write and sign some acknowledgments (such as 3.5) yourself; others (such as 3.9) you will prepare for your boss's signature. You will also need to prepare and send some acknowledgments (such as 3.3) in your boss's absence. Regardless of who writes or signs the letters, the format for most of them is simple and straightforward. Hence the models shown here can be stored in your computer file and readily adapted to fit each new situation. Chapter 13 gives examples of similar communications sent by memo, and the Model Selector Guide will direct you to models of more subject-specific acknowledgments in other chapters.)

Simple acknowledgments, such as confirming the receipt of an order, are almost always brief and easy to process. Models 3.1 to 3.9 are examples of simple acknowledgments of correspondence or material received.

The second type of acknowledgment—one that also answers a question—is slightly more involved and sometimes requires more thought to prepare. The question, for example, could necessitate some research to provide a suitable answer. Letters 3.10 to 3.16 provide some typical patterns for acknowledgments that also answer.

MAKING SIMPLE ACKNOWLEDGMENTS

A simple acknowledgment should not be considered unimportant just because it is basically straightforward and routine. Even the briefest, simplest acknowledgment conveys an impression of you and your company to the recipient.

1. Respond promptly.
2. Indicate what you received.
3. Express your appreciation for whatever you received.

The following nine models are examples of typical acknowledgments that respond without answering.

Information Received

3.1. With Document

Dear Julie:

Thanks very much for sending the sales report I requested. This will make it so much easier for us to prepare for the January board meeting.

I really appreciate your quick response--it all arrived just in time.

Best wishes,

When someone makes a helpful gesture and rushes something to you, he or she deserves a sincere expression of thanks.

Information Requested

3.2. You Send Document

Dear Mr. Davis:

We were delighted to learn about your interest in our consumer reports. The index you requested is enclosed.

I hope this will be helpful to you in selecting specific reports to order. Do let us know if we can offer any further information.

Thanks so much for your interest.

Sincerely,

Model 3.2 illustrates a standard procedure in acknowledgments of requests for information: Offer to supply additional information and thank the writer for his or her interest.

Personal Letter Received: Employer Is Away

3.3. Condolences

Dear Mr. Letterman:

Your letter announcing the untimely death of your associate James Ringley arrived while Mrs. Baxter is away on business. I know she will be deeply saddened by this unfortunate loss and will contact you immediately when she returns.

Sincerely,

This type of acknowledgment should be brief but have a sympathetic tone. It should state that your boss will respond as soon as he or she returns. (If a close friend of your boss dies, relay the message immediately by telephone.)

Business Letter Received: Employer Is Away

3.4. Transmittal Letter

Dear Mr. Hefner:

Since Mr. Putnam will be away from the office until March 23, I'm sending you the tapes you requested in his absence. As soon as he returns I'll ask him if there is any additional information we could provide. In the meantime, I hope the enclosed material will be useful.

If there is anything further I can do to help until Mr. Putnam returns, please let me know.

Sincerely,

Busy executives travel frequently and rely on their secretaries to acknowledge correspondence in their absence. Model 3.4 is a simple acknowledgment in the form of a transmittal letter sent while the executive is traveling. Typically, it promises to alert Mr. Putnam as soon as he returns.

Order Received

3.5. For Books

Dear Mr. Franklin:

Thank you for your order for twelve (12) of our Second Annual Conference Proceedings. I've forwarded all information to our publications office, and I know it will give your order prompt attention.

Sincerely,

Although most orders could be simply and efficiently acknowledged by form or filled promptly and sent by return mail, certain occasions warrant a personal acknowledgment. Model 3.5 concerns an order from an important member of the association; the opportunity is used to make personal contact with the member and strengthen the member-society relationship.

Order Changed

3.6. For Merchandise

Dear Mrs. Addler:

We'll be happy to change your recent order for Sesame Stoneware service for eight to service for twelve. I've forwarded this change to our warehouse, and you should soon be receiving your new service for twelve.

We appreciate your interest in these lovely dishes and hope you will enjoy them for many years.

Sincerely,

Model 3.6 illustrates how to use a simple acknowledgment of a change in an order to build customer relations.

Remittance Received

3.7. For Membership Renewal

Dear Mr. Phillips:

Thank you for sending your annual fee for membership renewal. We appreciate your continuing participation in the society and hope you will enjoy and benefit from the many new programs and activities scheduled for the coming year.

Sincerely,

Even the simple acknowledgment of a remittance, if made by an individually printed-out letter rather than a printed form, can be used as an opportunity to build goodwill and solidify relations. In this case the society chose to use a more personal approach rather than just send a membership card with an impersonal printed acknowledgment.

Appointment Requested

3.8. For Job Interview

Dear Ms. Harper:

Thank you very much for letting us know that you would like to find a suitable position at Newton College. Ellen Rossberg in the Personnel Office will be happy to see you to discuss your qualifications and current job opportunities at Newton.

Please telephone me at 643-0100 to set a date for an appointment.

Sincerely,

Model 3.8 is an example of the typical simple acknowledgment. It does not offer any information about positions that are open, nor does it comment on Ms. Harper's qualifications and prospects for finding a job at the college. It does not even specify the time or place for an appointment but rather asks Ms. Harper to telephone to make these arrangements later.

Confirmation of Verbal Agreement

3.9. To Serve on Committee

Dear Hal:

Thanks again for asking me to serve on the Entertainment Committee at the club next year. As I mentioned by telephone today, I don't foresee any complications in my schedule, so I'd be happy to serve on the committee.

I'll look forward to receiving details from you concerning the next meeting.

Best regards,

Although your boss would sign a letter such as this, you may be expected to write it.

SENDING ACKNOWLEDGMENTS THAT ALSO ANSWER

Some acknowledgments must also supply additional information. Such letters may need extra attention and care in preparation. The same rules used for a simple acknowledgment, however, apply here as well, and these letters also can be stored in the computer for recall and editing later.

1. Respond promptly.

2. Indicate what you received.

3. Provide as much information as you can to answer the letter or request.

4. Express appreciation if something is received.

Models 3.10 to 3.16 are examples of the pattern used to acknowledge and answer a letter.

Information Received

3.10. With Missing Item

Dear Ms. Block:

Thanks for letting me know that a detailed description of my property has been sent directly to a number of prospects. The address list was enclosed with your November 5 letter, but the property description was missing.

Would you please send me a copy of the description? I'd like very much to see it. Since I'll be leaving on vacation in a couple weeks I'd appreciate it if you could put it in the mail to me this week.

Cordially,

Letters calling attention to the omission of enclosures should describe what was and was not received. If the missing information is needed by a specific date, be certain to make this clear.

Personal Letter Received

3.11. With Congratulations

Dear Al:

I want to thank you for your thoughtful letter congratulating me on my recent interview in the <u>Brentwood News</u>. You're right--it was a welcome opportunity for me since the interview gave me a chance to say some things I've long believed about our increasing tax burden in Brentwood. I'm especially pleased to learn that you agree with my remarks.

I appreciate your vote of confidence, Al. Let's hope it all does some good!

Regards,

Model 3.11 is an example of a response that not only acknowledges someone's letter but uses the opportunity to confirm the writer's stand on an issue of importance.

Business Letter Received: Employer Is Away

3.12. About Speaking Engagement

Dear Mr. Ellis:

Thank you for reminding Ms. Webster about her promise to speak at your club luncheon on Wednesday, August 9. She's away on business now, but I know she's planning to return in time to address your group.

I'll bring your letter to her attention as soon as she returns, and I'm certain she will contact you promptly to confirm these arrangements.

Sincerely,

Model 3.12 is an example of a letter that tries to satisfy the writer but assures him that the intended recipient will soon respond personally.

Order Received

3.13. Send Apology for Delay in Filling

Dear Mrs. Prentiss:

Thank you for your order for twenty (20) 8 x 10 executive reminder calendars. Our previous supplier discontinued this line last month, and I regret that there will be a two- to three-week delay while we wait for a shipment from our new supplier.

The calendars should be here by October 12, and I'll telephone you immediately as soon as they arrive.

Please accept my apologies for this unavoidable delay.

Sincerely,

There could be a number of variations of model 3.13, which illustrates the personal contact that might be given to a good customer: a recommendation for a substitute calendar that might be available sooner, a promise to look for another source if the order is urgent, and so on. In any case, though, a letter would thank the customer, explain the delay, and offer an apology.

Remittance Received

3.14. With Error in Payment

Dear Mr. Addison:

Thank you for sending your payment of our invoice number 1-03295J for the electrical wiring work completed in July. We note, however, an overpayment: The amount due is $341.20; your check total is $347.20. Therefore, our check refunding the overpayment of $6.00 is enclosed.

We appreciated the opportunity to handle your electrical wiring needs and hope you'll call on us again when we can be of further service.

Sincerely,

Ordinarily, a remittance such as that described by model 3.14 would not be acknowledged by personal letter. The error in payment, however, made it necessary to acknowledge the payment and explain why a refund was due. If an underpayment had been made, it would be necessary to explain the difference between the total due and the payment enclosed. Depending on company policy, an invoice for the balance due might be enclosed, or a request for payment due might be made in the letter without enclosing an invoice.

Order Sent Incomplete

3.15. *You Suggest Substitute*

Dear Mrs. Pollock:

We are sorry that two of the items listed in your January 14 order are temporarily out of stock. The two-foot brass planter and the set of our walnut-grained trays have been back ordered and will be available after March 1.

Our winter sales flyer (copy enclosed) offers a variety of other planters and trays--all available immediately should you care to select substitutes for the out-of-stock items. Just let us know, and we'll change your order right away. In the meantime, the rest of the items you requested are being sent to you by UPS this week.

We sincerely regret the delay in filling part of your order. Thank you for your patience.

Cordially,

Model 3.15 concerns an acknowledgment that would not likely be made by personal letter if it were not desirable to use the occasion to build customer goodwill by explaining on a personal basis that substitutes for the originally ordered items are available. Notice that the letter also offers an apology.

Inquiry Received

3.16. *You Recommend Appointment*

Dear Ms. Sampson:

Although we expect our remote assembly control to be operational within one month, we haven't yet collected and published the information you requested.

One of our chief researchers, Rudolph Kraeger, has been supervising most of the developmental activity on this project and could answer many of your questions. You may reach him at 423-4001. If you would like to set up an appointment with Mr. Kraeger, please telephone me at 423-4000. I know that he would be happy to talk with you about the new control.

We appreciate your interest. Thanks very much for writing.

Sincerely,

An acknowledgment that only partially answers should advise the writer how or where to find further information. Model 3.16 is an example of a situation in which no published information is available. The only alternative source for immediate information, then, is a telephone or personal interview.

4

Reminders and Follow-ups

HOW nice it would be if all business letters were promptly acknowledged by their recipients. Since many letters are not always acknowledged in a timely fashion—or at all—reminders and follow-ups are an essential part of a secretary's daily correspondence. Usually, secretaries maintain follow-up files to alert them on which date, for each pending item, a follow-up or reminder must be sent.

You will send many reminders and follow-ups under your own signature (such as 4.7). Your boss will likely sign certain letters (such as 4.6), although you may draft them. Most reminders and follow-ups have a standard pattern, and it should be easy to maintain models in your computer file and tailor them to the requirements of each new situation. (The Model Selector Guide will lead you to other follow-up and reminder letters, such as "Writing Follow-up Sales Letters" in chapter 12, throughout the book. See also chapter 13 for follow-ups and reminders prepared in the memo format.)

Reminders are frequently sent to confirm plans previously made and acknowledged. Thus the reminder could cover almost any conceivable situation of this type, although the more common reminder letters concern appointments (4.1), meeting notices (4.2), invitations (4.6), expressions of interest (4.5), and requests for something (4.3 and 4.4). The reminder can also be considered a follow-up letter (such as 4.3), even though the stress is on reminding.

A follow-up letter could pertain to as many or even more situations as the reminder—virtually anything. Models 4.7 through 4.15 concern typical situations requiring a follow-up, such as an unreturned telephone call (4.8), a letter received with something missing (4.12), an invitation for someone to return after an interview (4.14), and an order never received (4.15).

SENDING REMINDERS

Reminders are usually brief, although occasionally a situation requires the repetition of numerous facts. In either case the letter must be specific. To be of any value, it must be sent in time for the recipient—who may have forgotten everything—to take whatever action was originally planned.

1. Specify the facts pertaining to the commitment (what is planned, when, and so on).
2. If pertinent, specify the date of the original commitment and whether it was made verbally or by letter.
3. If there is time, request a confirmation by letter or telephone.
4. Do *not* suggest that the recipient is thoughtless or forgetful.

The following six models are only a few of the possible circumstances requiring a reminder; as you will see, however, the tone and pattern of reminders is similar from letter to letter, even though the situation may change.

Appointment

4.1. For Business Luncheon

Dear Steve:

This is just a note to let you know that everything is set for our March 14 luncheon date at the Kingsley Inn. I have a table for five reserved in my name, and the others will meet us there at 12 o'clock.

I hope nothing has come up to affect these plans for you, Steve, but do call if you anticipate any problems in joining us. Otherwise, I'll look forward to seeing you then.

Best regards,

Model 4.1 would be appropriate if the plans were made far in advance and it is conceivable that someone may have forgotten the date in the meantime. Often such reminders are handled by telephone; if a person is very busy, however, it can be helpful to have something in writing. Dates and times are too easily confused and forgotten in telephone conversations.

Meeting Notice

4.2. For Club

Dear Lisa:

I hope you're still planning to be at our August 30 meeting of the Berkshire Club. We expect to start the meeting at 2 p.m. in the conference room at club headquarters.

Since I'm trying to estimate attendance now that the meeting date is almost here, I'd appreciate it if you could telephone me at 669-4000 or send me a note to confirm that you are still planning to attend.

Thanks very much, Lisa. Hope to see you then.

Cordially,

If you compare models 4.1 and 4.2 you can see how similar various types of reminders are even though the circumstances or events are different. In fact, many writers start all their reminder letters with the phrase "This is to remind you that . . ." As models 4.1 and 4.2 illustrate, however, there are other introductions that can be used to vary this type of correspondence.

Request Not Acknowledged

4.3. For Report Requested

Dear Mr. Field:

On March 7 I wrote to request twenty copies of your report <u>How to Sell with Visual Aids</u>, and your April 9 response stated that the copies would be sent shortly. As I indicated then, we want to distribute them at our June 1 sales meeting.

The reports have not yet arrived, but we are still interested in having them for use at the June 1 meeting. I'd appreciate it if you could let me know right away whether they will be delivered before that date.

Thank you.

Sincerely,

A reminder that involves a deadline should always ask for written acknowledgment by a certain date. Model 4.3, for instance, concerns a situation in which the reports *must* arrive before June 1, and the writer needs to know if this is not going to be possible.

Inquiry Not Acknowledged

4.4. For Information Requested

Dear Mrs. Wright:

I was wondering if you have had an opportunity to consider further my inquiry of August 5 about scanning equipment. You had replied that some literature would soon be on the way; however, the literature has not yet arrived, and we are still interested. In case my original letter has been mislaid, I'm enclosing a copy, which lists our requirements.

I'll look forward to hearing from you soon. Thanks very much.

Sincerely,

Two occasions when you might want to enclose a copy of your original letter are (1) when you suspect that the original was lost or (2) when the original contained numerous essential details you do not want to repeat in your reminder letter.

Expression of Interest

4.5. In Equipment Demonstration

Dear Bill:

Last fall, after stopping at your plant to see the model 420 computer in operation, I decided to wait until the 430 series was available before considering a purchase. You had suggested calling me later. Although I haven't heard from you, I was wondering if you now have the new 430 on the floor. If so, I would still be interested in a demonstration.

Please send a note or telephone me at 224-9360 as soon as you can arrange a private demonstration for me.

Thanks very much, Bill.

Regards,

Usually, sales representatives do not forget an interested customer or prospective customer. Occasionally, though, when considerable time has passed, it is necessary to send a reminder of your continuing interest. Model 4.5 closes by asking the recipient to acknowledge the letter—something that all reminders should do.

Invitation

4.6. To Workshop Panelist

Dear Mr. Shatner:

Have you had an opportunity to consider our invitation to you to participate in our training seminar as one of the workshop panelists on Tuesday, March 14, at 2 p.m.? I wanted to remind you that our deadline for the program is next Friday, February 5.

Because we haven't heard from you since extending the invitation last month, I'm wondering if my letter of invitation went astray. If so, please refer to the enclosed copy of my original letter, which contains full details regarding the workshop.

I sincerely hope you'll be able to participate; your contribution would add a great deal to the success of our seminar. Could you let me know this week so we can finalize our program? You can reach me at 245-7348.

Thanks very much.

Cordially,

When you write to jog the memory of someone who should have responded to an invitation, it is necessary either (1) to enclose the original letter or (2) to restate all details—date, time, place, type of event, and so on. If the details are extensive, it is easier to enclose a copy of the original.

THE FOLLOW-UP

All unanswered correspondence, telephone calls, invitations, orders, and so forth must be followed up at predetermined intervals. Usually, a secretary will check the follow-up file daily and send letters for everything still pending and due for follow-up on each day. The pattern of a follow-up letter is essentially the same as that for a reminder.

1. Specify all pertinent facts pertaining to the item or letter being traced.
2. Request a prompt reply to your letter.
3. Do *not* suggest that the recipient is thoughtless or forgetful.

Models 4.7 through 4.15 are only a few examples of the virtually endless variety of follow-up letters. The basic patterns shown in these models can be adapted to almost any situation requiring a follow-up.

Unanswered Letter

4.7. Of Request for Prices

Ladies and Gentlemen:

On August 16 I requested prices for your two dial-a-matic color heads for standard black and white enlargers. The information has not yet arrived, and we would like to have it as soon as possible so that we may place an order by the end of the month.

Could you send us the prices this week? Thank you.

Sincerely,

When you follow up this type of routine request for information, which is not directed to a particular person, it does not really matter whether you believe your original letter was lost or whether the company is just very slow in responding. Simply restate what you want as briefly as possible and specify when you need the information.

Unreturned Telephone Call

4.8. Of Request for Appointment

Dear Marge:

I wonder if you received my telephone message last week concerning a possible appointment for you to see Timothy Beal, manager, Courtland Supplies, Inc. Mr. Beal wants to expand his plastic container line, and I thought you might be able to discuss our products with him.

If you could send me a note or telephone me right away, I'll set up an appointment at the earliest possible date.

Thanks, Marge.

Cordially,

An unreturned telephone call can be irritating, but the tone of a follow-up letter in this situation must not show even a hint of annoyance. Simply restate what you wanted and ask for a quick reply.

Gift Not Acknowledged

4.9. *Holiday Expression*

Dear Ned:

I can imagine how busy you've been recently directing the opening of a new store in your territory during the hectic holiday season, so I thought I should check something with you. Two months ago today Roger and I sent you a gift--a hand-crafted paperweight --to wish you a happy holiday and congratulate you on the grand opening; I'm wondering if it perhaps went astray in the unavoidable confusion of moving to the new store.

Could you let me know if it arrived safely? If not, it was insured, and we can contact the post office here right away.

Best of luck with the new store, Ned.

Cordially,

After two months, a follow-up is in order when a gift has not been acknowledged. Model 4.9 suggests that the recipient has been extremely busy—something he can use as an excuse if he has just been tardy in sending a thank you. The letter also describes the gift in case it accidentally ended up on someone else's desk. Finally, the letter explains what can be done if it never arrived.

Inquiry from a Prospective Customer

4.10. *Interested in Merchandise*

Dear Mr. Vinson:

Last month you inquired about our new microcassette recorder, and I wanted to let you know immediately that a new shipment of these machines has arrived in our store. Would you like to come in and try one out?

The miniature version has most of the essential features of our standard model but because of its compact size can easily be carried in one's coat pocket. It is ideal for anyone who travels a great deal, and even in the office, executives enjoy its small, light-weight characteristics for handy desktop use.

I hope you can stop by soon to see for yourself how remarkable these new machines are. We're open from 9 to 5 o'clock Mondays through Saturdays. In the meantime, if you have any questions, just telephone me at 430-3900 or 430-6888.

Cordially,

Inquiries from prospective customers should be followed up as soon as possible by telephone or letter. In the situation described by model 4.10, it was necessary to wait until a shipment of machines arrived. Note that the follow-up letter is relatively brief but does some selling as well as relay the pertinent facts.

Following an Appointment

4.11. Company Hospitality

Dear Mr. Collins:

It was a thoroughly enjoyable experience to meet you and your associates last Friday and tour your plant facilities. I was very much impressed with your entire optical instruments manufacturing operation and thought the efficiency of your production crew was most remarkable.

Thank you also for the excellent lunch at your club. It gave me a chance to get better acquainted with your associates and learn more about our mutual interests.

I'll look forward to seeing you in Cincinnati next month at the precision optics conference.

Best wishes,

Successful business relationships are maintained by appropriate responses to all contacts. Thus a meeting where one executive enjoys the company hospitality extended by another must be followed up with a note of appreciation.

Transmittal Letter Received

4.12. With Missing Enclosure

Dear Mr. Jackson:

Since Mr. Ryan is away this week, I'm acknowledging your letter of January 30 to him.

You mentioned that you were including a tentative program for the Civic Center opening, but the program was not enclosed. If you could send a copy right away, I'll see that Mr. Ryan receives it just as soon as he returns next week.

Thanks very much.

Sincerely,

Letters with missing enclosures should be followed up immediately. One should never assume that the sender will later realize the omission and send the item.

Membership Application Received

4.13. Dues Not Enclosed

Dear Ms. Fredericks:

Thanks very much for completing an application for membership in the Lewistown's Secretarial Society. If you'll send us your remittance of $24 for one year's dues, we'll be happy to process your request for membership immediately.

Cordially,

When a remittance is not enclosed with an application (or order), there is no way of knowing if the sender forgot to include it or did not realize that payment in advance is required. Therefore, simply follow up promptly with a request for the amount due and state that the application (or order) will be processed promptly upon receipt.

Job Interview

4.14. You Ask Applicant to Return

Dear Mrs. Clark:

Mr. Baxter was pleased with your recent interview and application for the position of office manager.

Would you be able to come in again to discuss the position further with him? He will be free on Thursday, August 11, at 9:30 in the morning.

I'd appreciate a call at 463-1000 to let me know if this time is convenient. Thanks very much.

Cordially,

Follow-ups that concern an appointment must have the same ingredients as any letter regarding a specific date. Give the details regarding time, place, and so on, and ask the recipient to notify you if the time is convenient.

Order Never Received

4.15. *Supplies Needed Urgently*

Ladies and Gentlemen:

On March 21 I placed a rush order for two cartons of your black cartridge film ribbons, number 2245781. Since the ribbons have not yet arrived, I wonder if my original order went astray; if so, please consider this a duplicate.

We are urgently in need of replacements, so I would appreciate having this order sent immediately by United Parcel Service. The cartons should be delivered to our letterhead address, to the attention of Max Donnelley.

If these ribbons are out of stock or cannot be sent on a rush basis, please telephone me right away at 782-3011. Thank you.

Sincerely,

When you are following up on an order never received, take care in the wording of your letter. Notice that model 4.15 describes this as a *duplicate* order to avoid having it treated as a new, *additional* order for more ribbons.

5

Appointment Letters

ARRANGING appointments is an important part of a secretary's job. Although many plans for meetings and interviews are made by telephone, they are almost always confirmed by letter. Sometimes the appointment letter or your response to an appointment letter is the first impression that someone has of you or your company. Since first impressions are often lasting, it is essential that your letter be clear, accurate, and courteous.

In most offices the majority of appointment letters are written and signed by the secretary (such as 5.6). Even appointment letters signed by someone else are frequently written by the secretary (such as 5.10). Since appointment letters primarily concern details of time, place, and date, they are usually brief and straightforward. It should be easy, therefore, to change the basic facts and adapt the models in this chapter to your own needs. If you add them to your computer file of model letters, they can also be reedited to fit each succeeding situation. (Consult the Model Selector Guide for appointment letters in other chapters, such as 3.8 in chapter 3.)

Letters that make appointments can be grouped in two categories: (1) those that present all details without alternatives (5.1, 5.3, 5.5, and 5.6), the most common type of appointment letter; and (2) those that offer alternatives or leave certain details, such as the time, open (5.2 and 5.4).

Replies to requests for appointments vary more than letters making appointments. Some responses, for instance, grant the appointment

(5.7 and 5.8), some change or cancel the appointment (5.9 and 5.10), and others refuse the appointment either temporarily or indefinitely (5.11, 5.12, and 5.13).

MAKING APPOINTMENTS

Since appointment letters deal with facts such as time and place, they have to be accurate. Also, because the letters contain such specific information, they must be sent in time for the recipient to respond and comply with the suggested arrangements.

1. State the purpose of the appointment.
2. Suggest the time, place, and date.
3. Ask for a confirmation.

Just because letters making appointments must be factual and precise, however, they need not be abrupt and cold. Observe the pattern and tone of models 5.1 through 5.6, which represent the most common types of appointment letters.

Appointment for Your Employer: Time Set

5.1. To Make Presentation

Dear Mr. Boyd:

The enclosed walnut plaque is sent to you with our compliments. It's a sample from one of our recent shipments to Farnsworth Junior College. You'll notice it bears their seal in four colors.

Plaques such as this containing logos and seals are very popular with schools, clubs, and other groups. When produced in quantities of 100 or more, they are inexpensive and can be either awarded or sold at a profit by the purchasing organization.

We would like to show you more samples and tell you what we could offer your college. Would it be possible to visit your office? I will be in Houston on Monday, April 9, and could stop to see you at 3:30 p.m. Please let me know if that time would be convenient for you.

Thanks very much.

Cordially,

Model 5.1 asks for a response, presumably by mail. If time had been short, the letter could have asked for a fax or telephone response or could have said that someone would call the recipient on a certain date to confirm the arrangements.

Appointment for Your Employer: Time Open

5.2. For Plant Tour

Dear Mr. Winston:

Jeffrey Stevens, assistant production manager at Hill Market Services, will be in Detroit on Wednesday, August 13, and would like to have a tour of your plant while he is there.

Would it be possible for him to visit your facilities some time during the morning on Wednesday? Please let me know what time would be convenient.

Thank you very much.

Sincerely,

Some things such as a plant tour cannot be arranged at all imaginable times. Companies often conduct tours only on certain days at certain times. Model 5.2 requests a morning tour but does not ask for a particular hour, leaving it up to the company to specify the time.

Asking Someone to See Your Employer

5.3. About Budget Review

Dear Mrs. Kelly:

Mr. Brill would like to know if you could see him in his office on Tuesday, May 4, at 11 o'clock. He wants to review your recommendations for next year's budget.

I'd appreciate it if you would ask your secretary to telephone me at extension 511 to let me know if this time is convenient for you.

Thank you very much.

Sincerely,

Notice how the models of appointment letters all deal in some way with the four basic facts—time, date, place, and purpose of the appointment—and close with some comment regarding confirmation of the proposed appointment.

Requesting Appointment: With Alternative

5.4. For Choice of Location, Time

Dear Helen:

Would it be possible to meet with you for a half hour next week to discuss publicity plans for your upcoming warehouse sale? I have some ideas ready to present to you, and we could move ahead with the media as soon as the concept is selected.

Since we have a few materials that can't be transported easily, perhaps you would prefer to stop by our offices, say at 10:30 a.m. next Friday, November 9. If that isn't convenient, I could meet you in your office at 2 p.m. next Friday.

I'd appreciate a call from you as soon as you know which schedule would be most convenient for you. Thanks, Helen.

Cordially,

Sometimes there is a reason for offering an alternative for the appointment. In model 5.4 the writer wanted to mention that certain materials could not be easily transported; however, he also realized that some clients do not want to go to their supplier's establishment for an appointment, so he offered the alternative of calling on the client in her office.

Requesting Appointment: Without Alternative

5.5. In Employer's Office: Time Set

Dear Mrs. Lange:

Ms. Greenberg would like to know if you could come to her office at 3 o'clock on Tuesday, December 4, to discuss final arrangements for your children's trust fund.

Please let me know whether this time will be convenient for you. Thank you very much.

Sincerely,

Model 5.5 is a typical appointment letter. It specifies the time, date, and place without suggesting any alternatives. The letter nevertheless closes with a request to let the writer know if these arrangements are convenient. This letter assumes that the recipient is familiar with the location of the office where the appointment will take place; if that were not the case, the letter would have to give an address or further directions.

Confirming Appointment

5.6. To New Employee

Dear Ms. Maxwell:

Last week Mr. Benson suggested that you meet with him Monday morning, April 3, to discuss your new duties at Hillary Corporation. This is just to let you know that he is looking forward to seeing you in his office at 8:30 a.m.

Best wishes,

Model 5.6 is a confirmation of an appointment and thus does not ask the recipient to confirm the confirmation.

RESPONDING TO REQUESTS FOR APPOINTMENTS

The situation may be reversed in a reply to a request for an appointment, but the letter must still concentrate on the same basic facts of time, date, place, and reason for the appointment.

1. Repeat the essential facts of the appointment.
2. If the proposed appointment is inconvenient, suggest an alternative and ask for a reply.
3. If you must say no, do it politely.

Models 5.7 through 5.13 illustrate patterns to use in granting, changing, and canceling appointments.

Granting Appointment at Time Requested

5.7. To your Boss's Employer

Dear Mr. Bixby:

I'll be happy to meet you in your office on Wednesday, January 20, at 1 o'clock to discuss the Wilson report.

Regards,

There is no need for excessive detail or conversation in the confirmation letter. In this case your boss would sign the letter since it is going to his superior.

Granting Appointment at Time You Set

5.8. To Company Representative

Dear Phil:

I'll be glad to discuss the plans for our January inventory with you. How about meeting me in my office at 10:30 a.m., Tuesday, March 6?

Let me know if that time will be convenient for you. Thanks, Phil.

Best regards,

Even though model 5.8 is a confirmation, it suggests a time and therefore must conclude with a request for confirmation.

Changing Appointment

5.9. With Business Associate

Dear Morgan:

An unexpected complication in my schedule at the plant is going to prevent me from meeting you for lunch on Thursday, April 4. However, I'm free on Monday, April 8. Would it be convenient for you to meet me then at the Palmer House about 12:30 p.m.?

I'm sorry I can't keep our original date, but I hope Monday will be just as satisfactory for you. Could you have your secretary telephone my office to let me know?

Thanks very much, Morgan. I'm looking forward to seeing you soon.

Regards,

A letter changing appointments must briefly refer to the original appointment facts and specify the essential facts of the new appointment—time, date, place, and so on. The letter should also apologize for not keeping the original date and ask if the new arrangement is convenient.

Canceling Appointment

5.10. With Company Official

Dear Mr. Harris:

I'm very sorry to let you know that I'll be unable to keep our June 7 appointment to discuss the annual audit. Our West Coast office has been experiencing shipping problems, and the president has asked me to fly out immediately to lend a hand. Since it isn't clear right now when I can return, I'll have my secretary set up a new appointment with you next week.

My apologies for any inconvenience this may cause you, Mr. Harris. I'll be looking forward to our meeting later this month.

Cordially,

The cancellation letter should give—briefly—a reason for not keeping the appointment and apologize for any inconvenience caused by the cancellation. If the meeting must be rescheduled but a date can't be set at the time of writing, the letter should indicate that new arrangements will be made at a future date.

Refusing Appointment: Until Later

5.11. To Supplier

Dear Mr. Proxmire:

Thanks for letting Ms. Adams know that you have a new line of computer paper available for invoices and other forms. As much as she would like to see it, I'm sorry to let you know that because of previous commitments she won't be free for several weeks.

Perhaps you could mail some samples to her; if that is not possible, please telephone me at 921-0732 toward the end of this month to see how her schedule looks then.

Sincerely,

Model 5.11 is an example of a letter that says "No, not now, but perhaps later." A letter refusing an appointment, however, should not suggest the possibility of a later meeting unless you or your boss truly intend to see the person then.

Refusing Appointment: Indefinitely

5.12. To Overbearing Salesperson

Dear Mr. Billet:

Thank you for reminding us that you will be in town next week Wednesday and would like to discuss your printing services with Ms. McCarthy.

As Ms. McCarthy has indicated on several previous occasions, we are very pleased with our present arrangements for printing and definitely will not be considering any other services in the foreseeable future. Therefore, Ms. McCarthy has asked me to tell you that a meeting would not be helpful at this time.

We appreciate your interest, however, and thank you for writing.

Sincerely,

Some people do not easily take no for an answer, and it is necessary to become more firm with each refusal. Model 5.12 is an example of a refusal that is still reasonable friendly, although it clearly does say no. Businesspersons frequently try to leave the door open just a crack in case some day it will be necessary to do business with the person being turned away.

Refusing Appointment with a Suggestion

5.13. Referral to Another Department

Dear Ms. Javorsky:

Thank you for requesting an appointment to present your sample fabrics. This department, however, is not in charge of fabric selection. You might write to Mrs. Lorin MacDonald, purchasing coordinator, Room 410, at the letterhead address. I'm certain she will be happy to hear from you and will contact you about an appointment if she is in need of materials. In the meantime, I'll send your fabric samples to her office.

Thank you for writing to Ned's Apparel.

Cordially,

It is common business practice to refer people to another office whenever possible. This is helpful to everyone; in fact, it is a part of business life that people often need pointing in the right direction. Therefore, this type of appointment letter should always be friendly and informative, even though it says no to the immediate appointment request.

6

Introductions

and Recommendations

RECOMMENDATIONS and introductions can be difficult to write, primarily because they may involve an evaluation of someone's personal and professional characteristics. Such letters require diplomacy, tact, and honesty. What you say and how you say it may be critical both to the recipient and to the subject of the letter.

Because recommendations and introductions can be so sensitive (see, for example, 6.17), your boss may prefer to draft many of these letters but may expect you to refine and polish them. In some offices the secretary writes many of them (such as 6.8), although the secretary's boss signs them. You may also send certain letters (such as 6.12) under your own signature. Since practices differ widely from office to office, ask your boss which letters you should write and sign if you have any doubts.

Introductions, which you may give, request, or refuse, can involve individuals or organizations, friends or strangers. They may concern social or business situations, personal or professional characteristics. In short, introductions may vary greatly. Fortunately, there are basic guidelines you can follow in all types of introductions, as illustrated in models 6.1 through 6.10. Although the situations requiring the letters may vary considerably, add the models to your computer file so that you can recall them for editing in future situations that are similar. (Check the Model Selector Guide for examples of other correspondence pertaining to introductions, such as 8.7 in chapter 8.)

Letters of recommendation or reference, including those requested, given, and refused, are also varied and numerous. Often they concern financial and business matters (6.11 and 6.12), but one of the most familiar types of recommendation or reference, and the one that many secretaries will encounter most frequently, is the employment reference (6.13-6.19); thus chapter 6 offers a variety of models for these letters. Although recommendations and references, like introductions, differ according to circumstances, most of them employ a basic pattern you can use for the letters you write in your own office.

HANDLING INTRODUCTIONS

A letter of introduction can be sent along with the subject of the letter or, when time permits, mailed in advance. If it can be sent before the person's arrival, it gives the recipient a chance to refuse the introduction. Since you are really asking a favor of the recipient, it is only common courtesy to give him or her an opportunity to say no.

1. Provide whatever basic information will be useful about the person being introduced.
2. Explain why the recipient might want to meet the subject.
3. Give the recipient an opportunity to decline.
4. Thank the recipient.

Models 6.1 through 6.10 are examples of letters requesting, granting, and refusing introductions. If you are agreeing to meet someone, be appreciative; if you are refusing to meet someone or refusing to make an introduction, be tactful.

Requesting an Introduction: Business

6.1. To Prospective Client

Dear Bob:

Last Friday my boss gave me a challenging new assignment--to approach the Midtown Dental Supply Company as a prospective client for our public relations services. I thought of you right away since Wilson's president, Carl Edson, was your college roommate.

I was wondering if you could write a brief letter of introduction for me. I'll be in Chicago on July 12 and in a couple weeks plan to request an appointment with Mr. Edson. But I thought it would be helpful if a letter of introduction reached him first.

If you can find time in your busy schedule to do this--and wouldn't feel you were imposing on your old college friend--I'd certainly appreciate it. Thanks a million, Bob.

Best regards,

When you ask someone to write an introduction letter, explain why and when you want to see the person. Conclude with an expression of appreciation.

Requesting an Introduction: Social

6.2. For Club Membership

Dear Jim:

For several months Annette and I have been thinking about joining the Belmont Country Club. Since you and Marge have been members for many years, we were wondering if you could introduce us by letter to the president, Donald Whipple.

It probably isn't essential to have a letter of introduction precede us, but we are new in town. It might be reassuring to Mr. Whipple to know that "someone out there" has heard of us and can vouch that we don't rob banks or burn books!

If you can find a moment to do this and wouldn't mind, Annette and I would be most grateful. Thanks ever so much, Jim.

Cordially,

Although model 6.2 concerns a social situation, notice how similar the pattern is to that of model 6.1, which involves a business matter.

Introducing a Personal Friend

6.3. To Business Associate

Dear Pamela:

One of my dearest friends, Adele Stahl, will be in Boulder the week of June 5. She's such an enjoyable person that I'd like very much for you to meet her, so I've suggested that she telephone you some time that week.

Adele is the head designer at Litman, Parnell, and Benjamin in New York. Since you oversee the design staff at Rocky Mountain Creations, I know you both would have a good time comparing notes.

I'd appreciate any courtesy you can extend to Adele, although we'll both understand if your prior commitments will make it impossible for the two of you to get together.

All good wishes.

Cordially,

In any introduction, keep in mind that you are asking a favor and the recipient may not want to comply—thus the "out" offered in the third paragraph of model 6.3.

Introducing a Business or Professional Associate

6.4. To Prospective Employer

Dear Mrs. Nichols:

It's a pleasure to introduce Mike Ritter to you as a possible candidate for a position with your firm. I understand that he will be contacting you soon to request an interview.

Mike is presently employed at Holt Chemical Laboratories as a supervisor. We previously worked together before I left Holt to move to the West Coast. During the five years of our association, he was the perfect employee--responsible, highly capable, and a thoroughly delightful person to know.

I'd appreciate any consideration you can extend to him. Thanks very much, Mrs. Nichols.

Sincerely,

The pattern for a letter introducing a business associate is similar to that for a friend; however, you can see that the tone of model 6.4 is more reserved than that in model 6.3.

Introducing a Business Organization

6.5. *To Colleague*

Dear Bill:

Let me introduce to you the Medallion Uniform Service--an organization that could be of assistance to your company. We've been using Medallion services in Madison for seven years and have been completely satisfied with their continuing ability to provide low-cost, high-quality service. I've heard similar reports from other Medallion customers, for example, Madison Discount Mart and the Midwestern Bottle Capping Company.

A representative from Medallion will telephone you next week to ask for an appointment to discuss what they can offer your company. In case you are interested in learning more about them, I'm enclosing one of the brochures they recently left with me. I'm certain you would be pleased with their services.

Hope to see you soon, Bill.

Best regards,

A letter introducing a company should comment on the quality of its product or service and name a few of its customers. If it is not obvious, the letter should also indicate why the recipient might be interested in the company. (Notice that some letters of introduction also qualify as letters of recommendation and vice versa.)

Introducing a Job Applicant

6.6. *To Department Manager*

Dear Mr. Olmsted:

I'd like to introduce Sandra Birney to you as a possible candidate for a secretarial position in your department. I understand you have two openings in the secretarial-administrative area.

Sandra has been working in our Scranton office for four years, but as you know, we are terminating this facility on August 1. Considering her excellent training, solid secretarial and administrative experience, and pleasant personality, she would be a fine addition to your staff, and she is willing to relocate to Pittsburgh.

Since we are eager to find new positions for all employees left job-less by our branch closing, I'd appreciate any consideration you can extend to Sandra. I've asked her to telephone you next week to inquire about a possible interview.

Thanks very much, Mr. Olmsted.

Sincerely,

As model 6.6 illustrates, a letter introducing a job applicant should refer to the candidate's previous experience and personal character. Although if time is short the letter can be sent along with the candidate, it is usually desirable to mail or fax it in advance to give the recipient time to consider it.

Introducing a Sales Representative

6.7. To New Customer

Dear Mr. Solomon:

Nichols Wax Company is pleased to introduce Charles Wagner, our new representative in the Washington-Baltimore region. Charles has a thorough understanding of the problems and requirements in floor cleaning, maintenance, and refinishing for businesses. He is well quali-fied to discuss with you your needs in this area, and I know you'll enjoy his friendly, helpful attitude.

Charles will telephone you soon for an appointment to stop by and meet you personally. I hope you'll be able to see him then. If you need anything in the meantime, however, you can reach him at 202-661-7000.

Cordially,

The tone of the letter is important in correspondence that introduces a sales representative. The letter must convincingly suggest that the customer would enjoy and benefit from talking to the salesperson. If the letter pushes too much, the customer might react adversely and refuse to see the representative.

Introducing a Successor

6.8. *For Retiring Executive*

Dear Ethel:

It's a pleasure to introduce to you our new manager of quality control, Tom Walters. He is succeeding Earl Steiner who retired last week.

Tom will soon be visiting our Phoenix branch, and I know he'll want to meet you and learn about your cutting and stamping work. You'll enjoy his enthusiastic approach to everything he does. Tom is an intelligent and dedicated organizer, and somehow everything and everyone functions better when he is around.

You can be expecting a call or letter from his secretary very soon to let you know when he'll arrive. I'd appreciate it if you would welcome Tom and brief him on your operation.

Thanks very much, Ethel.

Cordially,

Two types of letters introduce a successor in business: a general introduction to all employees and an individual letter to specific employees, such as model 6.8. The general letter would be similar except that instead of asking a specific person to assist the successor, it would ask everyone to welcome and assist the successor.

Company Policy Prohibits

6.9. *For Former Employee*

Dear Ms. Russell:

As much as I would like to provide the letter of introduction you requested, I'm very sorry to let you know that company policy prohibits this practice.

Because we use so many part-time and temporary employees, it is difficult for us to get to know everyone as fully as we should. We thus limit our comments to standard replies to requests from companies for references. As an alternative to the letter of introduction, I would suggest that you have your prospective employers submit routine inquiries to my office, and I'll be happy to respond to them.

Please accept our good wishes for much success in finding a suitable position.

Sincerely,

Model 6.9 is an example of a letter that says no politely. Following the typical pattern for this type of letter, it offers a reason for the refusal, suggests an alternative, and closes by wishing the recipient good luck.

Cannot Justify the Introduction

6.10. For Troublesome Candidate

Dear Mr. Attleboro:

I'm sorry I cannot provide the letter of introduction you requested. Since your employment with our company was terminated because of the serious consequences of your behavior on the job, it would not be appropriate for me to write a letter on your behalf that ignored this problem.

Nevertheless, I sincerely hope you will benefit from past experience and overcome your difficulties. With determination, I'm sure you can achieve success in a suitable new position.

Sincerely yours,

Model 6.10 concerns a situation in which the person requesting a letter of introduction was fired because of serious trouble he caused. The writer, therefore, has refused to give him a letter of introduction, because he believes it would be unethical to comment without mentioning the problem. This is a highly sensitive type of letter. Although it firmly says no, a final paragraph is added to temper the harshness of the refusal and, it is hoped, to encourage the recipient not to give up but to do better in his next position. Any such statement, however, must avoid a pious, preachy tone, which would only antagonize the recipient.

HANDLING RECOMMENDATIONS AND REFERENCES

Letters of recommendation and reference, like letters of introduction, require diplomacy, tact, and honesty. Since they comment on the character and ability of a person (or organization), they can be sensitive and must be skillfully composed.

1. Provide information that will be helpful to the person receiving the letter of recommendation or reference.

2. Be as objective and honest as possible in your comments, but also be considerate in the way you say something.

3. If you are requesting a recommendation or reference, express your appreciation.

Although letters of recommendation and reference often need careful thought and planning, a basic pattern can be followed in the majority of cases, as illustrated in models 6.11 through 6.19.

Requesting a Bank Reference

6.11. For Business Loan

Dear Ms. Brunatelli:

Michael Dudley has applied for a business loan with us and has given the First National Bank as a reference. His application states that he has both a regular checking account and an interest-bearing account at your bank.

I'd appreciate knowing how long he has had these accounts and what the balances average in each account.

Thanks very much for your help.

Cordially,

A request for a bank reference usually mentions the type of account(s) and asks for (1) the length of time the applicant has had the account(s) and (2) the average balance in the account(s). (Often standard fill-in forms are used to request or give such information.)

Requesting a Credit Reference

6.12. For New Customer

Dear Mr. Forgione:

Wendall Smith and Associates has requested that we extend credit terms to them on future purchases of supplies from us. Donald

Travis, general manager of the firm, has given the name of your company as a credit reference.

I'd appreciate it if you would comment on their performance in honoring such commitments. Your comments and recommendations will be held in the strictest confidence.

Thanks very much for your assistance.

Sincerely,

As models 6.11 and 6.12 illustrate, requests for references concerning finances are similar. The first paragraph indicates who the applicant is and what the applicant's relationship is to the person or firm receiving the request. The second paragraph indicates what type of information is desired, and the final paragraph concludes with a brief word of appreciation.

Requesting a Reference from Former Employer

6.13. For Job Applicant

Dear Mrs. Whiteside:

Carol Brogran, one of your former employees, has applied for a secretarial position in our Training Division and has given your name as a reference.

I'd appreciate it if you could tell us something about her experience and ability. Your comments will be held in the strictest confidence.

Thanks very much for your help.

Cordially,

Sometimes firms enclose a form that makes it easier for the recipient to reply. Paragraph 2 might then read: "I'd appreciate it if you would use the enclosed form to comment on her ability and experience," or a sentence might simply be added: "A form for your convenience in replying is enclosed."

Giving an Employment Reference: Business

6.14. About Former Employee

Dear Mr. Wyatt:

Mary Kennedy was employed as our office manager for nine months in 1990 before she left to join another organization. Although her stay with us was brief, we were pleased with her performance. Her secretarial and administrative skills were excellent, and her capabilities in working with and supervising other employees were outstanding. She acted responsibly and conscientiously at all times, and we were sorry to have her leave so soon.

It's a pleasure to recommend Mrs. Kennedy as a valuable addition to the appropriate organization.

Sincerely,

A recommendation must always be honest. Model 6.14 acknowledges that the candidate did not stay very long with the writer's firm, although in every other respect she was an ideal employee.

Giving an Employment Reference: Personal

6.15. About Former Student

Dear Mr. Wilcox:

Robert Andretti entered Morgantown University in 1986 and received the bachelor of arts degree in economics in 1990. During that time he was a student in three of my social science classes.

I would heartily recommend Robert for the position you described. Although I'm not familiar with his employment record, I can assure you that he was a model student: creative, intelligent, well organized, and cooperative. With his friendly manner and congenial personality, it was always a pleasure to have him in my classes.

Let me know if I can do anything further to help.

Cordially,

The personal recommendation is similar to the employment recommendation in format. The principal difference is that the stress is on the candidate's personal characteristics with little or no indication of his business background.

Open Letter of Recommendation

6.16. About Colleague

To Whom It May Concern

I'm pleased to have this opportunity to comment on the important contribution Matthew Miida made to the success of Royal Advertising Associates. For five years he was responsible for all of our art production, including each stage of preparation from concept to mechanical.

In spite of the great variety of literature we handled--magazines, newsletters, books, catalogs, posters, brochures, ads--he was able to apply his extraordinary talent and broad experience in each instance, enabling us to serve many different types of clients. Mr. Miida is a truly gifted artist, and I have great respect for his high-quality work and his responsible and trustworthy character.

Matthew Miida would be an asset to any firm concerned with the preparation of artwork. I believe the appropriate organization would benefit immensely from his contribution.

Sincerely yours,

The open letter of recommendation follows a pattern similar to that of any other recommendation and should be honest and informative. Headings vary; some firms object to the general "To Whom It May Concern" greeting and use something more specific such as "To All Prospective Employers."

Refusing to Provide Reference

6.17. For Difficult Former Employee

Dear Mr. Bronx:

I'm sorry to let you know that I cannot provide the letter of reference you requested. Your employment record with us was unsatisfactory, and it is our policy in these situations not to furnish such letters. However, I personally wish you luck in finding more satisfying and successful employment elsewhere.

Sincerely,

The refusal to provide a recommendation or reference is similar to the refusal to provide a letter of introduction (model 6.10). Although you must say no firmly if circumstances require it, such as they do in model 6.17, your letter should not anger the former employee or discourage him from trying to be successful in a new position.

Thank You for Employment Reference: Position Accepted

6.18. By Job Applicant

Dear Ms. Eddington:

Your letter of recommendation to Mr. Colter was so effective that I have been offered the position of administrative assistant. It's a wonderful opportunity, and I intend to accept the offer immediately.

Thanks for all your help. I really appreciate it.

Sincerely,

Thank yous for references can be brief. Model 6.18 typically acknowledges how important the letter of recommendation was and expresses genuine appreciation for it.

Thank You for Employment Reference: Position Declined

6.19. By Job Applicant

Dear Mr. Trilling:

I want you to know how much I appreciated your recent letter of recommendation to the Boston Wentworth Corporation. Although they did offer me a position, it was not quite what I was looking for. I have therefore decided to decline it and continue looking for something more suitable.

I hope I may continue to use your name as a reference. Thanks so much for all your help, Mr. Trilling.

Sincerely,

Even though positions are not found or are not accepted, it is only common courtesy to thank someone who has written a letter on your behalf. Model 6.19 expresses appreciation, explains that the job offer was not accepted, and mentions that further letters of recommendation may be needed.

7

Employees

THE day-to-day operations of an organization are affected to a great extent by the quality of its internal business communications. Although a substantial portion of internal communication is handled verbally or by memo (see part II), a surprising number of employee situations are best handled in the traditional letter format. Sometimes the writer wants to personalize the correspondence as much as possible or perhaps give it a more thoughtful, formal appearance than the memo would provide. At these times the memo might appear too general, too informal, or too hasty a form of communication. Regardless of whether the communication is prepared in memo or letter format, most companies will send it by means of interoffice mail, thus avoiding the cost of postage.

You will write some letters in this chapter specifically for your boss's signature (such as 7.14), and others you may write and sign yourself (such as 7.19). When you prepare employee letters for someone else's signature, the extent to which you write or rewrite depends on the practice in your office. Perhaps your boss relies on you to draft most of these letters, merely supplying the facts to you; if the letter concerns a highly sensitive situation, perhaps your boss prefers to give you a rough draft, which you refine and polish. Although the major facts may change in each situation, many of the letters (such as 7.1 and 7.6) will be repeated over and over. Others may be used less often but also may be needed on certain future occasions. In any case, include the models in your computer file for recall later.

Motivational letters are common in many companies, particularly in those that have more than just a few employees. Although individually these letters serve a specific purpose (such as thanking an employee for something), generally, they serve to motivate employees by increasing their job satisfaction and encouraging them to work harder and perform better. Examples of motivational letters to employees are welcome letters (7.1), thank you letters (7.2, 7.3, and 7.9), letters promoting support and unity (7.4, 7.5, and 7.6), apologies (7.7), and letters of advice (7.8, 7.10, and 7.11).

Some situations necessitate criticism, not commendation, and sometimes it is necessary to say no tactfully but firmly. Letters of rejection require special attention because they must accomplish a specific purpose without antagonizing or discouraging employees and thus adversely affecting their future performance. Examples of such letters are refusals to give something (7.14), rejections of something offered (7.12 and 7.19), criticisms (7.17 and 7.18), and refusals to accept responsibility for something (7.20). (Consult the Model Sector Guide for similar nonemployee models found in other chapters throughout the book.)

SENDING MOTIVATIONAL LETTERS

The most important thing to remember in writing a motivational letter is not what to say but what *not* to do.

1. Avoid any appearance of beating a drum or lecturing from a soapbox.

2. Do not get so carried away with lavish compliments that you sound insincere.

If you make a point honestly and thoughtfully, your letter stands a much better chance of inspiring and motivating the employee. The eleven models that follow are examples of the wide variety of motivational employee letters commonly written in the modern business office. Although you will be substituting your own facts and figures in each situation, you can retain the simple, straightforward style and the smooth, conversational tone the models project.

Letter to New Employee

7.1. Welcome

Dear Bob:

It's a pleasure to welcome you to the new training center at A. G. Harvey Chemical Corporation. With your extensive background in industrial training, I'm certain you will find numerous opportunities to use your many talents and capabilities.

You will soon meet the rest of our "family" at the center, and I know you won't be disappointed. They all share your enthusiasm for thorough and constructive training procedures, and their dedication is matched by their enjoyment of the special sense of fellowship we share at the center.

Remember, my office is just down the hall from yours. Stop by any time, and do let me know if I can answer any questions about your duties or help you become better acquainted with the training center.

Best regards,

The welcome letter is the most common type of letter to new employees. It is usually intended as a friendly gesture, with either management or an employee saying hello and welcome to another employee and offering to be of assistance to the newcomer. This type of welcome letter is brief and does not go into detail about job duties or company rules and regulations.

Thank You Letter: Group

7.2. For Special Effort

Dear Staff Members:

It comes as no surprise to me that Samuels & Davis Company just completed its spring shipments on time--in spite of our recent equipment problems. With all of you devoting 200 percent of your time and energies to emergency adjustments and rescheduling difficulties, how could we fail?

I'm truly impressed by your unhesitating efforts on behalf of the company and want to extend my gratitude to each of you. I know this past month has been a difficult time--long hours, late hours, and weekends away from your families. But without this united effort, we would never have been able to satisfy all our customers, and as you know, the loss of even one customer would have had an adverse impact. Thanks to you, however, our customers received their merchandise on schedule, and operations are back to normal.

The loyalty and devotion you displayed over an extended period merit the highest commendation, and I have made arrangements for each of you to receive a special citation at our annual awards banquet. Samuels & Davis Company can truly be proud of its employees. My sincere thanks for your selfless and generous contributions.

Cordially,

This type of thank you letter stresses the employees' unselfish devotion to the company. The sincere praise gives them a desire to continue to make contributions.

Thank You Letter: Individual

7.3. For Suggestion

Dear Jeanne:

Your suggestion to cut rising production costs by estimating and combining our orders for stock with other departments is precisely what we need. I think you've found a realistic way to trim our somewhat strained budget this quarter, and the potential savings should appeal to other departments as well.

If ever you have any further thoughts on ways to improve our operating procedures, please send them along. New ideas are always welcome in this department; in fact, constructive suggestions are of benefit to the entire company.

For all of us--thank you!

Sincerely,

In model 7.3 the writer thanks the employee for a particular contribution and specifically asks for further contributions.

Encouraging Employee Support

7.4. For New Policy

Dear Jerry:

Now that registration has nearly ended for our four-week, in-house training program, it is clear that participation may fall short of our expectations. We believe that the small turnout is in part the result of our failure to communicate fully to each employee the important benefits of this new evening program. As training manager, you will have an opportunity to discuss the program personally with many of the employees.

As you know, Reynolds Data Processing Company would like you to conduct a brief training session twice this year on a voluntary-participation basis, free of charge to all employees. It's an excellent opportunity for employees to increase their knowledge in this expanding field and prepare themselves for advancement--all without cost and with a minimum of effort. It will undoubtedly bring some employees a step closer to promotion and a salary increase. As a side benefit, the program will provide a chance for employees to get to know each other better and to make new friends as they share a very pleasant and highly interesting hour together twice a week next month. Those who finish the program will have a better understanding of the service that Reynolds provides and their function in the company in relation to others.

If the program succeeds, it will be Reynolds' policy to offer in-house training sessions similar to this each year. We'll need your help and the help of many others to make this possible. Please visit the various departments and let the employees know about the exciting possibilities of this program and how the investment of just a few hours of their time can produce substantial dividends for them later.

Sincerely,

Letters encouraging support sometimes require more detail than others. The recipient should never be asked to support something blindly; the reasons should be summarized in the body of the letter clearly and logically, followed by the request for support and assistance.

Letters That Unify

7.5. *Stimulating Company Pride*

Dear Staff Members:

I just received some exciting news for all of us at the House of Fashion--for the third successive year we have been asked to present a one-hour fashion show at the State Merchandising Association's annual convention!

You are all aware that competition in our industry is fierce; it is a distinct honor to be chosen again and again by one of the state's most prestigious associations. Since House of Fashion's success is really <u>your</u> success, I know you must be as thrilled as I am that the results of our mutual efforts throughout the year continue to be recognized and rewarded.

I am delighted to be part of a winning team and hope we will continue to work together to keep House of Fashion at the forefront.

Cordially,

The object of this letter is to stir up enthusiasm for the company. One sure way to arouse enthusiasm in others is to be enthusiastic yourself.

New Year's Resolution

7.6. *About Performance*

Dear Staff Member:

Have you ever thought that New Year's resolutions are silly because no one keeps them anyway? I have, but the truth is that not all resolutions are silly, and not all of them are broken. To the contrary, a realistic and worthwhile resolution can and should be kept at any time of the year.

I've decided to take the plunge again this year--how about you? To be certain I won't make my resolutions on January 1 and break them on January 2, I've made my list both simple and sensible. For instance, I haven't vowed to work a ten-hour day instead of an eight-hour day, because it's not important whether I sit in my office eight or ten hours. But how much I accomplish when I'm there is important. If I can perform better, I might be able to do more in eight hours than I would otherwise do in ten.

I'd like to invite you to join me in this effort to improve performance. Somehow I think it will be easier for each of us to keep our resolutions if our coworkers have the same objectives. Then when it's time to share in the rewards, we will all feel we have truly earned them.

I'm genuinely looking forward to working with you this coming year. Please accept my thanks for your good work in days past and my best wishes for success and prosperity in days to come.

Happy New Year!

New Year's letters are usually of two types: a brief, simple greeting or a greeting combined with a call to greater and better things. Model 7.6 uses the occasion to motivate the employee to perform better in the future. To avoid having the letter end up in the wastebasket, the writer uses the second paragraph to add a realistic, down-to-earth tone before asking the employee to make a resolution in the third paragraph.

Response to Motivational Letter: Apology

7.7. About Misunderstanding

Dear Heather:

You're absolutely right--my project report is due this Friday, the 14th, and I'm embarrassed to say that I haven't yet finished it. In haste, I had erroneously noted on my calendar that it would be due next Friday, the 21st. Although I've been pursuing a frantic appointment schedule for nearly a month, I don't know how I could have confused the dates. I'm very sorry.

I'll start working on the rest of the report today and guarantee it will be on your desk by next Tuesday. In the meantime, is there something else I could do to alleviate any problems my tardiness may have caused? Please let me know.

I appreciate your patience, Heather--thanks so much.

Cordially,

This positive response to a motivational letter concerning a deadline follows a sound rule in business: If you're wrong, admit it, apologize, and make amends. An apology must try to lessen the frustration you may have caused the other person.

Advice to Employee

7.8. About Company Benefits

Dear Employee:

I'm proud to report that each year Marc Davis, Incorporated, has increased the number of benefits available to its employees. Last month a brochure describing current employee services was circulated in all departments, and by now you have had a chance to read about our programs and raise questions about your personal participation in them.

I urge you to review our company programs again and think about each one in terms of its applicability to you. Ask yourself if you are really receiving all the benefits to which you are entitled and, if you are not, why not. Perhaps you have not completed the necessary forms, or perhaps the extent of services available to you is not clear. For example, are you taking advantage of our matching-funds tuition plan? Are you using our free, volunteer medical services—X-rays, eye examinations, and so on?

If you have any questions about whether you are receiving all benefits available to you, write to our director of personnel services, Jerome Hanley, immediately. If your questions cannot be answered by mail, Mr. Hanley will be glad to see you to discuss our employee services in detail. Simply telephone his secretary, Ms. Jackson, at extension 2396 for an appointment.

I sincerely hope you will continue to enjoy and profit from the ever-expanding roster of company benefits at Marc Davis.

With warmest regards,

It is often necessary to give advice to employees; such letters must make it clear why the employees will benefit from taking the advice. If the letter proposes specific action, instructions must also be stated clearly, as for example in the third paragraph of model 7.8.

Increase in Salary

7.9. As Reward for Productivity

Dear Frank:

It's always a pleasure to extend some tangible evidence of our appreciation for a job well done. Yes, your increase in salary from $35,800 to $38,000 a year has been approved! It will become effective January 1.

I can't think of anyone who deserves a raise more than you. I know you have an excellent team, but it's largely through your innovative efforts and good judgment that productivity in your department broke all records this year. You may be certain that your accomplishments have been duly noted, and we're all grateful for your contribution to the company.

Congratulations on the raise, Frank. Keep up the good work.

Best regards,

See chapter 8 for other letters that use expressions of congratulations and goodwill to motivate employees.

Giving Advice: Employee Requested

7.10. About Difficult Assignment

Dear Jan:

I hope you were exaggerating when you said that you were having second thoughts about your latest assignment. It's going to be a tough job to reorganize administrative services, but I really believe you can handle it.

I'm flattered that you asked for my opinion, especially since the assignment sounds so familiar. My own department was having similar problems a few years ago--an increasing staff and decreasing productivity. We needed not more people but more efficient people. After streamlining operations, certain positions simply were not justified, and a staff reduction seemed mandatory. I'm not qualified to make a judgment about your department, but if you've concluded that a staff reduction is absolutely essential, I think you should make the recommendation without hesitation--along with suggestions for transfers to other departments when possible. It's not easy to suggest that some jobs be eliminated, but it's also not fair to the others to have someone on the payroll who isn't making a contribution. In time, your staff would resent that even more than they would object to staff dismissals.

If you'd like to discuss this further, Jan, why don't we have lunch some time this week? You know I'd be happy to help any way I can. Call me and we'll set a date.

Cordially,

There is one thing to guard against in letters giving advice—being held responsible later if something goes wrong. Notice the safety valve in the letter above: "I'm not qualified to make a judgment about your department," meaning, "It's your decision; please don't blame me if it doesn't turn out right."

Giving Advice: Without Being Asked

7.11. To Assistant

> Dear Polly:
>
> It's good to see the progress you've made in setting up our office library. We're all eagerly waiting for the rest of the publications to arrive.
>
> Have you had an opportunity yet to devise a checkout system? I noticed someone from the sales office removing a book this morning without signing it out. This could become a problem as borrowing increases and books disappear from the shelves without any indication where they've gone. I know you're pressed for time now, so how about working up a temporary checkout system to tide us over until something more official can be established?
>
> Let me know if you have any questions, Polly, and thanks for doing such a fine job with our long-awaited library.
>
> Best wishes,

Model 7.11 has a mild criticism in the advice, softened with a compliment and rendered gently so that the assistant will not be hurt or discouraged.

WRITING LETTERS OF REJECTION

Letters to employees that say no must be written with special care. No one likes to receive a refusal, and feelings can be hurt if the rejection is not presented with tact and consideration for the recipient. It does not help, however, to beat around the bush or try to soften the blow with insincere compliments.

1. If something is offered, such as a suggestion, thank the employee.
2. Tell him or her why—gently but firmly—it cannot be accepted.
3. If possible, give the employee some encouragement for future efforts.

It is extremely important to avoid discouraging the employee. A discontented and possibly humiliated person would not likely perform well in the future and possibly would not even stay with the company.

The next nine letters are examples of employee letters that reject something. Since they cover the most familiar situations of this type, you can easily use your own facts and adapt each one to your specific situation.

Rejecting a Proposal

7.12. *Of Business Associate*

Dear Tom:

I read with great interest your proposal to expand our field operations. Thanks for taking time to present this idea. Although it sounds like an excellent plan, I'm sorry we can't take advantage of it now.

As you know, we're making preparations to introduce several new household products, and recent figures indicate that this operation is going to draw on all of our available resources for the next eight months. We just wouldn't have the capital, labor, or training capability to broaden our territory now. But if the new products are successful, this could open doors, and your plan might then be ideal. You may be certain I'll remember your suggestion if the right time comes.

I wish I would receive more good ideas like yours. It would make my job a lot easier. Thanks, Tom.

Best regards,

If the proposal in model 7.12 is totally unrealistic for now and the future as well, the slant of the letter will have to be changed to avoid any suggestion of future use. The complimentary and appreciative tone should remain in any case.

Rejecting Request for Meeting

7.13. *Insufficient Information*

Dear Russ:

I've been considering your request for a staff meeting where you could present your idea for a monthly "suggestion roundtable."

Although this idea sounds interesting, I hesitate to schedule a full staff meeting without knowing a little more about your proposal. Could you send me a synopsis of your plan--summary of idea, specific benefits, for whom, who would be involved, and so on.

I'll look forward to learning more about the proposed "suggestion roundtable." After I've had a chance to study the idea, I'll let you know if it appears that a meeting would be useful. In the meantime, please accept my sincere thanks for developing a new idea to improve employee performance. This type of creative thinking is a tremendous asset to our company.

Best regards,

This model thanks and compliments the employee but makes it clear that the immediate request is denied (and tells why); it does not make a commitment for the future one way or another, pending receipt of more information.

Refusing to Give Raise

7.14. Because of Budget Restraints

Dear Mr. Steiner:

Although your record at Letterman, Inc., is satisfactory, and the company appreciates your interest in making further contributions, current budget restraints prevent us from making any salary increases. All salaries in your division are scheduled for review in six months, however, and you will be notified if there is any change in conditions then.

In the meantime, I hope you will continue to enjoy your work at Letterman.

Sincerely,

If the employee's record had been more distinguished, the tone of this letter probably would have been raised to indicate that a raise in the future is very likely. However, even though Mr. Steiner has not won any medals for outstanding performance, the company does not want to discourage him and cause him to perform poorly or quit.

Termination of Employee Contract: Financial Reasons

7.15. Budget Cuts

Dear Ms. Fosdick:

We are very sorry to let you know that, because of budget cuts, your services with Goldmeier Metalworking must be terminated effective April 1, 19__.

The management decision in implementing budget cuts was to eliminate five positions in your division. The termination will affect support staff and trainee personnel, which includes your position.

This decision was in no way influenced by your performance, which has been excellent. We sincerely regret that this action could not be avoided, and we wish you success in finding another position. You may be certain that we will provide a good reference for you should you require it.

With best wishes,

Letters releasing an employee are difficult to write. In model 7.15 the employee had a good record at the company, so the writer closes with wishes for success and an offer to write a good reference.

Termination of Employee Contract: Conduct

7.16. *Absenteeism*

Dear Mr. Bendor:

The management of Porter Foods, Inc., hereby requests your resignation effective August 11, 19__.

It is company policy that excessive absenteeism to the point that an employee can no longer perform his or her duties effectively requires this action. Although your supervisor has discussed the problem of absenteeism with you on numerous occasions, the situation has not changed.

We hope that you will take appropriate steps to correct this problem so that you may soon find a suitable and rewarding position.

Sincerely,

Most companies proceed with caution in terminating employees for performance-related problems. When in doubt concerning laws covering employee and management rights, consult an attorney.

Criticism of Employee: Individual

7.17. *About Performance*

Dear Mr. Rydell:

The board has completed its review of your activities and expenditures during the past six months. Generally, we believe you have met most of our expectations satisfactorily. There is one matter, however, that we would like to discuss with you.

Although you did not exceed the allotted budget for the past quarter, we notice that you used surplus funds to make to business trips to San Francisco and Montreal. Your stated objective was to solicit memberships in the association and sell copies of our manual. We strongly believe this is a poor investment of time and funds. It is not economical to spend more than $1,500 a week on travel in an effort to sell some $3 manuals; nor is it wise to spend $200 an evening taking interested persons out on the town in hopes of receiving one or two $15 memberships in return.

I'd appreciate it if you would make arrangements for an Executive Committee meeting within the next few weeks. Specifically, we would like to discuss (1) more efficient and economical ways to promote membership and sell publications and (2) the more advantageous use of surplus funds. I'll look forward to hearing your suggestions at the meeting.

Regards,

This type of letter concerns a sensitive situation, which means that your boss will probably draft it. The objective is to reprimand Mr. Rydell but give him a second chance and avoid hard feelings in the process. Thus the last paragraph states that at the meeting the discussion will focus on future procedures, not on the pros and cons of Mr. Rydell's travel and entertainment expenditures.

Criticism of Employees: Group

7.18. About Conduct

Dear Employees:

Yesterday afternoon, in the scramble to leave work at 5 o'clock, an employee's car struck the car of a customer in our parking lot. Although damage was minor and no one was injured, this customer was astounded at the wild and rude behavior of our employees, who were dangerously and carelessly speeding away.

It is entirely possible that we will lose an important customer as a result of this objectionable behavior, but something that concerns me even more is the threat to the safety of all persons, whether customers, employees, or innocent bystanders. This reckless behavior must cease immediately, and I am requesting that each employee in this company observe all rules of common courtesy in the presence of others and--at all times--act with full regard for the safety and well-being of others. If voluntary cooperation is not sufficient to provide a safe atmosphere for everyone, I will have no choice but to impose a strong regulatory measure.

I hope the next report I receive will be quite different. Although not all employees were guilty in this instance, we all can benefit from a greater awareness of the serious consequences that confront us when we forget the basic rules of common courtesy and consideration.

Yours sincerely,

The writer in model 7.18 decided to issue a stern reprimand but give everyone a chance to improve his or her own conduct before imposing harsh restrictions.

Declining Offer of Help

7.19. On Committee Assignment

Dear George:

I appreciated your offer to help me with the committee's resource survey. It's good to know that someone out there wouldn't mind giving up tennis for a few Saturdays!

Everything is off to a good start, however, and if I don't hit any snags, I'll be able to finish without imposing on anyone else to help. But if the situation changes, you'll be the first to know! Thanks for the offer, George.

Best personal regards,

Refusal to Accept Responsibility for Problem

7.20. In Letter to Superior

Dear Mr. Johnson:

I was distressed to learn that our city services proposal was denied because it was based on an advocacy position. When I prepared it, I was under the impression that this was the position held at headquarters in New York.

The instructions I received (photocopy enclosed) say nothing about funding being contingent on a pro and con approach. As you can see, these instructions came from our New York office. No doubt the original instructions from the Endowment Fund, which probably contained the pro-con clause, were retained at headquarters.

If you would agree to it, I would be glad to write a new proposal for a study of both sides of the city services issue. This time, however, I think it would be a good idea if I received a copy of the Endowment Fund's instructions, along with the guidelines from headquarters.

Please let me know if I should proceed with a new proposal.

Sincerely,

Any refusal to accept responsibility for something must clearly state why—and the reason(s) must be adequate. If possible, the letter should close with some gesture to help correct the situation anyway. If the letter blames someone else, great care must be taken. Harsh, perhaps inaccurate, accusations can lead to trouble and even lawsuits. Letter 7.20 avoids blaming any individual and merely makes an explanation without specifically criticizing someone else.

8

Appreciation and Goodwill

COMMUNICATION in the business world goes far beyond activities that affect the exchange of goods and services. Whatever the ultimate business purpose may be, people must deal with people. Thus letters that influence the feelings and attitudes of others are of critical importance. Successful public relations is greatly dependent on the effectiveness of letters of appreciation and goodwill; although these letters are usually brief and easy to compose, their importance should not be underestimated.

You can easily write the majority of these letters (such as 8.6), although your boss may sign many of them. Occasionally, your boss may feel better qualified to draft the basic letter but will leave it up to you to polish it (such 8.16). In either case, these letters are rarely complex, and you should find it relatively simple to use the models in this chapter as your guide. Keep them on file in your computer for future use. (Refer to the Model Selector Guide for similar models throughout the book, such as 6.18 in chapter 6.)

In the business world you can never send too many letters of appreciation. Few letters are so warmly received and so effective in promoting good human relations. Models 8.1 through 8.16 are examples of the numerous occasions that warrant an appreciative response.

Successful public relations is a highly desirable goal of any organization, and letters of goodwill are vital in building public confidence and encouraging favorable attitudes toward your company. Many situations can be used for this purpose, from sending holiday wishes (8.17 and 8.18) to offering praise for a worthy suggestion (8.20 and 8.21).

The letter of congratulations is a very distinct type of goodwill letter. Although it is often very personal and thus effective in cementing business friendships, it is also highly effective as a tool in building good public relations for the company. Models 8.24 through 8.32 reveal how letters of congratulations can create feelings of goodwill among individuals and organizations.

SENDING LETTERS OF APPRECIATION

Some people have difficulty expressing themselves warmly in a letter; others fall into the opposite trap of becoming too flowery and gushy. Letters of appreciation will sound insincere if they are too restrained or too overflowing.

1. Be natural and sincere in your expression of appreciation.
2. Explain why you appreciate what was done.
3. If appropriate, offer to reciprocate.
4. Also, if appropriate, encourage the recipient to contribute further.

Letters of appreciation can be sent in response to any situation in which someone does something thoughtful or commendable. The following sixteen models are examples of the many situations that would warrant letters of appreciation.

Prompt Payment

8.1. By New Customer

Dear Mr. Willis:

I want to thank you for your letter and remittance for our recent landscaping work. It was a pleasure to be of service to you, and I sincerely appreciate your prompt payment.

If we can be of further help in planning and maintaining your lovely resort grounds, please do let me know. I'll look forward to hearing from you again.

Cordially,

Although you would not write a personal letter to thank everyone who pays a bill, some businesses use this occasion to build good relations with a promising new customer. The letter should express appreciation for the prompt payment and indicate that it was a pleasure to be of service.

Personal Favor

8.2. By Business Associate

Dear Brad:

I sincerely appreciated your help in completing our proposal for a new wing at the recreation center. Without your assistance I would certainly have missed the deadline. But thanks to you we made it, and I'm very confident that the proposal is a good one and will be adopted.

If ever I can reciprocate, Brad, just let me know.

Best regards,

Like most letters of appreciation, a letter commenting on a favor can be brief. It should sincerely express gratitude and offer to reciprocate.

Offer of Assistance to Firm

8.3. By Colleague

Dear Roy:

It is very thoughtful of you to offer to take over my three evening classes so that I can attend the machine tool show in Chicago next month. I had planned to cancel them as a last resort, but if you can fill in, it will be so much better.

I'll telephone you next week to set a time for us to go over the lesson plans together. Thanks a million, Roy.

Best regards,

The letter of appreciation for an offer of assistance (1) expresses gratitude, (2) accepts or rejects the offer, and (3) suggests the next step if the offer is accepted.

Message of Congratulations

8.4. Upon Election

Dear Mr. Johnson:

Thank you so much, Mr. Johnson, for your kind letter of congratulations and warm wishes. It was good to hear that you supported the environmental protectionist stand that led to my election to the Barkley Society Board of Directors. With your help and that of all others who believe in our cause, my job will be much easier.

Cordially,

Responses to letters of congratulation will vary slightly depending on whether the situation involves a new job, an award or honor, or something else. In all cases, though, a *brief* expression of appreciation is usually preferable, unless the writer is seeking additional support or has some other reason to comment further on his or her achievement.

Message of Sympathy

8.5. Upon Death of Spouse

Dear Edna:

Thank you for your thoughtful expression of sympathy and offer of assistance. Marie considered you one of her dearest friends. Your kind words were very comforting, and I appreciate knowing that I can call on you if the need should arise.

Sincerely,

Letters of appreciation should always be sent in response to expressions of sympathy. Replies usually are very brief—no more than one to three sentences.

Favorable Mention

8.6. In Article

Dear Mr. Fenton:

I was surprised and pleased to read the flattering remarks about my recent Community College address in your article "The Last of the Pioneers." Your books and articles always--and justifiably--have an extensive readership, so I'm especially happy to know that you approve of my universalist philosophy.

My sincere thanks, Mr. Fenton.

Cordially,

A letter of appreciation for complimentary remarks should indicate where you read or heard the remarks and what they referred to and offer thanks for the favorable mention.

Introduction

8.7. To Prospective Client

Dear Fred:

I just talked to the purchasing manager at Crystal Distributors, and he would like to see me next week! Since he mentioned your name, it's obvious that your letter of introduction opened the door for me.

Thanks ever so much, Fred. I truly appreciate your effort and hope I can be of help to you some day.

Best regards,

Model 8.7 is a typical appreciation letter. It refers to the recipient's effort, tells why the act was appreciated, gives thanks for it, and offers to reciprocate.

Receiving Advice

8.8. From Subordinate

Dear Angela:

I think you should be the first to know that our looseleaf service is a huge success; after all, you were one of the first to recommend publishing our market studies in this format. Fortunately, we all had sense enough to realize that your advice was right on target.

I'm making a point to let others around the office know about your important contribution. For now, Angela, please accept my sincerest thanks.

Best wishes,

Sometimes writers include a sentence in letters encouraging the recipient to contribute further, such as "Keep up the good work" or "Any further ideas you have will be most welcome."

Hospitality: Overnight Guest

8.9. Of Business Associate

Dear John:

Thanks for a delightful weekend with you and Janet. I so much enjoyed visiting with both of you in your home, and those wonderful meals were a very special treat for me. You must give me a chance to reciprocate the next time you're in Buffalo.

My best to Janet.

Cordially,

Acknowledgments of hospitality, like all appreciation letters, are brief. Since they often concern thanks for personal attention, the letters frequently have an especially warm and personal tone.

Hospitality: Dinner Guest

8.10. Of Business Associate

Dear Ken:

Thank you so much for that splendid dinner at the Carriage Inn last Thursday. The meal was outstanding and the conversation stimulating--an unbeatable combination.

It was good to see you again, and I'll be looking forward to our next meeting.

Best regards,

Conference Speaker

8.11. An Invited Guest

Dear Mrs. Kline:

Thank you for your generous comments about my speech at the Eastern Merchants' conference. It was a pleasure to appear before this distinguished group, and I'm pleased to know that my remarks were meaningful in some way.

Sincerely,

This type of appreciation letter would vary depending on the recipient. If the letter were directed to the person who had originally invited the speaker, for example, it would also have to express thanks for that invitation, even though, presumably, a thank you letter for that purpose was sent earlier.

Invitation to Open House

8.12. Of Supplier

Dear Mr. Ripley:

Thank you for the invitation to your open house and buffet on Wednesday, March 11, at 12:30 p.m., in your new offices in Kansas City. It will be a pleasure to help you celebrate the opening, and I'll look forward to seeing you then.

Cordially,

This informal type of thank you for an invitation would be appropriate if the invitation is also informal (such as a letter invitation). If it had been formal, the reply also would have to adopt the formal style (see model 15.8 in chapter 15).

Bonus Received

8.13. A Special Reward

Dear Mr. Severin:

I was delighted to receive your letter telling me that a bonus would be forthcoming for my work on the Benson project. Thanks ever so much.

The project was challenging, and I'm happy that I had the opportunity to tackle it. Although I never dreamed a bonus was in store, you may be certain it is most welcome. Mrs. Franklin and I truly appreciate the company's generosity.

Many thanks, Mr. Severin.

Cordially,

A letter of appreciation for a bonus or salary increase must obviously express sincere thanks. Sometimes the writer refers to his or her spouse's gratitude as well. If the bonus is a reward for doing something special, it also should briefly acknowledge the activity and indicate that it was a pleasure to make the contribution.

After a Company Tour

8.14. With a Client

Dear Mr. Hollister:

Thank you again for arranging such an informative tour of your company. I'm confident that I have a much better understanding of your activities in Louisville and that this will enable us to improve our service to you.

I sincerely appreciated your time and thoughtful attention, Mr. Hollister and now will look forward to having you visit our facilities in Deerfield.

Best regards,

Model 8.14 concerns a tour of a client's establishment; thus it includes a statement of how the knowledge gained will help the writer's company provide better service. The general thank you for a tour would be almost the same, except that it should omit this statement and might also omit the concluding suggestion that the tour host visit the writer's facilities.

Thank You with Request

8.15. For Favor

Dear Ms. Godine:

Your layouts for our spring catalog just arrived, and they look absolutely marvelous! Thanks for working so hard to keep our tight production schedule.

Although I'm completely satisfied with the layouts, I wonder if you could do one more thing--design a tearout insert to be placed just inside the back cover (copy enclosed). This is something that came up at our staff meeting yesterday afternoon, and I just received the copy this morning. Fortunately, it will be a separate piece that won't disturb the other pages. I'd really appreciate it if you could get the design for this insert to me by the end of this week.

Many thanks for your usual good work, Ms. Godine. We're all very pleased.

Cordially,

When you must include a request for something in your letter of appreciation, be certain that the request does not totally overwhelm the expression of gratitude. Preferably, begin and conclude the letter with words of appreciation, keeping the request in a middle paragraph.

Thank You with Rejection

8.16. *Of Work Unacceptable*

Dear Mr. Lewis:

As much as I appreciate your promptness in filling our June 17 order for 4,000 invoices and matching window envelopes, I regret that we cannot accept the finished product.

If you'll compare the ink on the enclosed new invoice with that of the letterhead paper on which this letter is written, you'll notice a distinct difference in color. Although we might have been willing to live with a slight variation, this extreme change would cause problems since all of our materials--invoices, brochures, stationery, and so on--are color matched. I don't know what caused this problem; possibly in the rush the ink was not mixed correctly.

I'm sorry to bring you this news. Perhaps the paper itself can be retained and portions of it cut for later use as small memo or note paper. We will be placing an order for these items in August. In the meantime, I'd appreciate a call from you as soon as possible to discuss replacing the invoice order.

Thanks very much, Mr. Lewis.

Sincerely,

A thank you letter that includes a rejection will either reject something with no request for replacement, or it will say no but ask for a corrected version. Although model 8.16 rejects an order, the writer has no desire to end his relationship with the supplier. The letter expresses appreciation for the supplier's promptness, and the mild tone of it indicates that the supplier is thought to be a fair and cooperative person. If this were not the case, the letter would place more stress on the error and build a case that the supplier could not avoid. Either way, a letter such as this should never display anger or frustration but should be civil and businesslike.

WRITING GOODWILL LETTERS

Individually, goodwill letters serve many purposes, but in general they are used to build good public relations. The essence of a goodwill letter is its attitude, and the writer should keep this guideline foremost in his or her mind.

1. Use an appropriate occasion to say something thoughtful or flattering.
2. When you offer something, do not ask for or expect an immediate favor or reward in return.
3. Be natural; write warmly and sincerely, but without excess.

Models 8.17 through 8.23 illustrate a few of the countless occasions that can be used to send a letter of goodwill.

Holiday-Seasonal Greetings: Customer

8.17. To Longtime Customer

Dear Frank:

During the holiday season I'm always reminded of the many things for which we at Porter Industries can be grateful. At the top of our list every year is the fine relationship we enjoy with good customers like you.

This is the eleventh year we've been doing business with you--can you believe it? I know I've enjoyed every year and look forward to many more. In particular, it's always a pleasure to work with you, Frank.

All of us at Porter send you and your associates our very best wishes for a beautiful and bountiful holiday season.

Cordially,

Holidays are perfect occasions for letters of goodwill. A letter to a customer should comment on the good business relationship and close with holiday greetings. Except for a friendly remark about looking forward to many more years of friendship or good business relations, such a letter should *not* become commercial and try to do some selling on the side.

Holiday-Seasonal Greetings: Employee

8.18. To All Employees

Dear Employee:

This has been a busy and exciting year for all of us at Browning and Beale. Thanks to your loyal and dedicated efforts, we have much to look forward to in the coming year.

Although we're not a large company, we have gained solidarity and strength through our many friendships and our cooperative spirit. I feel very proud and happy to have you on our team, and I hope we will be able to make your position at Browning and Beale more satisfying and rewarding each year.

Warmest regards to you and yours over this holiday season, and my sincerest wishes for a peaceful and plentiful New Year.

Cordially,

Holiday greetings to employees vary from brief letters of good wishes to more involved commentaries on the employee's participation in the company's progress. Some focus on the subject of New Year's resolutions (see model 7.6 in chapter 7).

Tribute to Employee

8.19. A Retiring Worker

Dear Staff Member:

It's both my sad and my pleasant duty to let you know that our maintenance engineer, Gerald Fitzpatrick, has reached that enviable position of independence--retirement.

Although we will miss having Gerald just around the corner ready to solve all our problems, we know he has earned the right to do his own thing. I can't think of anyone who has been more essential to our daily operations. Gerald has been our link between go and no-go for nearly thirty years. It's astounding to recall how many times his superb maintenance skills and know-how have kept us from disaster.

Let's hope he doesn't go too far away to hear a sudden cry for help! But in the meantime, why don't you join me in sending him your warm wishes as he embarks on his new life of freedom and leisure.

Cordially,

The tribute to an employee is a general letter of praise sent to other employees or business associates. If this were an individual letter to the retiring employee, it would follow the same general pattern and tone, except the remarks of praise and good wishes would be personally directed to the employee.

Commend Suggestion, with Rejection

8.20. Of Assistant

Dear Louise:

I was fascinated with your suggestion for a departmental newsletter. Thanks so much for your thoughtful plan. I'd like to consider the idea again a little farther down the road. At present our staff time and resources are too limited for us to add an extracurricular activity, but we all hope that situation will eventually improve.

For now, I just wanted you to know how much I appreciate your suggestion. In fact, creative and imaginative ideas like yours are always welcome. Many thanks, Louise.

Best wishes,

A rejection will not build goodwill unless the tone is clearly one of appreciation and encouragement in spite of the refusal. Model 8.20 downplays the fact that it is saying no by beginning and ending the letter with a warm expression of thanks and particularly flattering remarks. Whenever possible, *all* situations should be used to encourage and improve human relations.

Commend Suggestion, with Acceptance

8.21. Of Assistant

Dear Dick:

That was a great idea of yours to have our printer ribbons reinked rather than discard them. I placed an order this morning with a local service, and you are right--the savings will amount to $2.50 a ribbon, which will be very significant over a year's time.

Your excellent suggestion is going to be of real benefit to the company, Dick. Many thanks for your help.

Best regards,

Model 8.21 adopts the same general approach as most other goodwill letters. It uses a newly accepted idea as an opportunity to build good human relations by complimenting the assistant who suggested it.

Letter with Gift

8.22. To Customer

Dear Ms. Anderson:

Now that we've completed photographic coverage of your fifth annual conference, I want you to know how grateful we are for the opportunity to provide this service to you each year. Please accept the enclosed personalized photo album as a small token of our appreciation.

Sincerest thanks for your confidence in us, Ms. Anderson. It's always a pleasure to work with you.

Cordially,

A letter to a customer with a genuine gift—not a sales gimmick or product sample—should offer the gift with a sincere expression of appreciation of warm wishes. This type of letter, however, should *not* try to sell anything. (Whether gifts may be given or accepted, however, depends on company policy.)

Free Offer with No Strings

8.23. To Prospective Customer

Dear Mr. Kirby:

Since we're practically neighbors now, I want to welcome you to Sunset Hills on behalf of all of us at Neil's Dry Cleaning Service Center.

We know the first few weeks after moving into a new community can be a difficult time. There are always a million things to do and lots of unexpected expenses. Clothes and dry goods sometimes arrive wrinkled, dusty, and soiled. Because we know this so well, we'd like to make your move a little easier for you. Here, with our compliments, are five coupons that will permit you to have up to fourteen garments or other items dry-cleaned free of charge within the next three weeks.

If there's anything else we can do to make your introduction to Sunset Hills more enjoyable, all you have to do is call. We're delighted to have you as our neighbor and look forward to meeting you soon.

Cordially,

Notice that model 8.23 does not qualify the offer. It is completely free with no strings attached. Although the writer hopes the recipient will patronize his or her establishment, the immediate objective is to build goodwill.

SENDING LETTERS OF CONGRATULATIONS

People respond positively to praise and recognition. Because of this, letters of congratulations can be a valuable tool in a businessperson's efforts to win goodwill.

1. Write sincerely and enthusiastically, without evidence of envy.
2. Devote your comments to the recipient's accomplishments and do not make other remarks that would overshadow it.

Situations that warrant letters of congratulations are innumerable, both in business and social situations. Models 8.24 through 8.32 are examples of some of these occasions.

Award Given

8.24. To Employee

Dear Jim:

Congratulations! I was so pleased to read in the paper this morning that you had received the Lovett Award for Outstanding Community Service. I've followed your relentless efforts to beautify our downtown shopping area for two years, and it's clear that you've been our champion from the very start. We at Gibson Tool Company are happy and proud to know that one of our employees has received such as coveted award.

You truly deserve this recognition of your generous and invaluable contribution, Jim. I don't know what we--or Lovett--would do without you!

Regards,

The length and content of a congratulatory letter will differ with the occasion. However, model 8.24 illustrates one thing that should be repeated in all such letters--the spirit of unselfish, enthusiastic praise for the recipient.

Promotion

8.25. Of Business Associate

Dear Ted:

I was delighted to learn about your promotion--congratulations! You've certainly earned it, and I know you'll find your new responsibilities exciting and challenging.

Best wishes, for success in the new position, Ted.

Cordially,

Most letters congratulating someone upon promotion are brief, the purpose being simply to offer congratulations, say that he or she deserves the promotion, and wish the person well in the new position.

Banquet Address

8.26. Of Guest Speaker

Dear Mr. Hollingsworth:

Let me congratulate you on making one of the finest speeches that members of our organization have ever had the privilege of hearing. The audience was practically spellbound by your astute analysis of small business failure in America. I thought the applause would go on all night when you presented your five-point plan for progress.

Your ideas are ingenious, and I want to thank you sincerely for sharing them with us. We hope you'll join us soon again as our guest at a future luncheon.

Cordially,

Whether a letter to a guest speaker is sent as a congratulatory note or a straight thank you letter depends on the circumstances. Model 8.26 concerns a situation in which the speaker deserved a word of congratulations for developing and presenting a particularly clever plan.

Outstanding Contribution

8.27. *For Community Service*

Dear Leonard:

You must be very proud of your recent success in prodding community leaders to take a tougher stand on law and order. Without
your courageous citizen's campaign to control vandalism and street
crime, I believe we would be even worse off today than we were
a year ago. But thanks to you, the proper authorities are acting to
reverse the alarming trend we've experienced.

There may not be a specific medal available for your contribution,
but you have unquestionably won the gratitude of those of us who
live in Ridgeway. Because of your persistent efforts we all feel much
safer on the streets today.

Sincerest congratulations, Leonard, for a job well done.

Regards,

Model 8.27 illustrates a key point to remember in deciding when
congratulatory letters can be sent. Expressions of commendation
and praised are appropriate whenever someone makes a contribution,
whether or not the effort is publicly acknowledged and whether or
not any award has been bestowed.

Business Anniversary

8.28. *Of Customer*

Dear Mr. Jarvis:

It's a pleasure to send you our sincerest congratulations on the sil-
ver anniversary of Ramsey Builders. We at Logan Lumber Company
consider it our good fortune to have had you as a customer for
the last ten of those twenty-five years.

It is common knowledge that Ramsey Builders is one of the most respected firms in this part of the country. You truly have something
to celebrate on this occasion; from its birth, your firm has made
steady progress and growth, winning countless friends in every
sphere of the business world along the way.

We look forward to Ramsey Builders' next twenty-five years and
wish all of you the great success and satisfaction you so richly deserve.

Cordially,

In a congratulatory letter to a customer it would be easy to stray from the purpose of the letter and stress your relationship with and your service to that customer. But this must be strictly avoided. As model 8.28 illustrates, the remarks should focus on the customer's time of glory.

Business Achievement

8.29. A New Development

Dear Ms. Arnold:

During a visit to the lab yesterday I had an opportunity to see your new test gauge in use. It's a magnificent instrument! You must be proud, indeed, to know that this highly useful tool is your own creation. Its accuracy is amazing, and it is surprisingly easy to use. How exciting to think of the many potential applications for it outside as well as inside the classroom.

Sincerest congratulations on this remarkable achievement, Ms. Arnold. Your work is an inspiration to all of us.

Best wishes,

A congratulatory letter concerning a new development (new product, new service) should be enthusiastic and comment intelligently, even if briefly, on it. In model 8.29 the writer took time to learn a few basic facts about the new gauge—its accuracy, ease of use, and numerous potential applications. Such remarks make it appear that the writer is truly interested in the new development.

New Business

8.30. Of Former Employee

Dear Stan:

How wonderful it was to learn that your new agency is open and ready for business--congratulations! With your experience and proven capability in advertising, I know your organization will be a huge success.

My very best to you, Stan. I'm so pleased that all your good work has paid off.

Cordially,

One thing always to guard against in writing letters acknowledging the good fortune of others—letting a hint of envy creep into the letter. This can happen unintentionally. For example, a remark such as "some people have all the luck" could be made in good humor, but the recipient might mistake it for sour grapes.

On Marriage

8.31. Employer's Assistant

Dear Joe:

Edna and I send you our sincerest congratulations on your upcoming marriage. Our very best wishes to both of you now and in the years to come.

Cordially,

Although marriage congratulations can be as brief as model 8.31, they will vary depending on how well one knows the recipient, whether one is invited to the wedding, and so on. Model 8.31 would be suitable in most instances.

Commend Performance

8.32. Employee Recognition

Dear Jane:

Congratulations on doing such a beautiful job redecorating our offices. I knew you were talented and creative, but this time I think you even broke your own record! I can hardly wait for more people to visit so that we can show off the results of your hard work.

Thanks a million, Jane. I love all of it.

Best wishes,

As you can see from model 8.32, many letters are really a combination of appreciation and congratulations. This model focuses on congratulations for outstanding work but closes with a word of thanks.

9

Social-Business

Messages

BUSINESS and social activities inevitably overlap at times, and circumstances often require a social-business letter or invitation. Sometimes this letter is sent on special letterhead that is usually smaller than standard business stationery (consult printers and stationery stores for samples). Although social-business correspondence is more personal than other types of business communication, and is thus effective in building business friendships, it is also an excellent means to build favorable public relations for your company. The secretary plays a key role in helping to maintain good social-business relations by recognizing and pointing out occasions when such a letter or invitation would be appropriate. (See chapter 15 for models of formal invitations.)

Although your boss will sign the majority of these letters, you may draft most of them (such as 9.1). Some letters you may also send under your own signature (such as 9.11). The models in this chapter follow a standard pattern that can be used in composing these letters; however, as you substitute your own facts, take care to retain the warm, personal tone that should characterize most of these letters. If you keep them in your computer file of models, they can be edited on screen when future occasions arise. (Consult the Model Selector Guide for models of social-business correspondence in other chapters.)

Most invitations are issued by letter, as models 9.1 through 9.6 illustrate. This informal style of communication is typically used for invitations to lunch, dinner, a party, an open house, and so on. It is also common in soliciting memberships in professional societies, requesting donations, and asking someone to speak at a special event.

Replies to informal invitations are also sent by letter. Models 9.7 through 9.12 are examples of the style and tone to follow in accepting or declining invitations. Most replies will be either an acceptance or a refusal; occasionally, though, your boss may decide to accept after first refusing or vice versa (see 9.12).

In addition to preparing the specific invitation or reply to an invitation, the secretary regularly handles miscellaneous letters for social occasions. Although a list of potential situations would be endless, models 9.13 through 9.21 concern many common social occasions: expressions regarding birthdays, holidays, thank yous, condolences, gifts—generally, any special event.

ISSUING INFORMAL INVITATIONS

Once you have determined that an informal letter invitation is appropriate for the occasion in question, the next step is to decide exactly how informal the tone of the letter should be. The tone of a letter asking a friend to have lunch would be more casual and personal than that of a letter to a prominent person asking him or her to address a conference.

1. Specify what the occasion is, such as a dinner.
2. Indicate the reason for the invitation, such as to celebrate an anniversary.
3. Specify all details about the event, such as time, place, and who will be there.
4. Request a reply by a certain date.

Letters of invitation are appropriate for many occasions; models 9.1 through 9.6 illustrate the pattern and tone to use in composing these letters.

Luncheon Invitation

9.1. To Business Associate

Dear Henry:

Would you be able to have lunch with me on Monday, June 9? If you're free, I'd like to have you be my guest at the Harcourt Inn.

My associate Jim Kimberly will also be there, and we plan to meet about 12:30 p.m. in the cocktail lounge. Jim, you may recall, is the engineer you met at our offices last month. He's still fascinated with your new building designs!

Let me know if you can join us, Henry. I hope you can. Jim and I are both eager to see you again.

Cordially,

Model 9.1 is a typical letter of invitation to someone the writer knows well—hence the casual tone.

Party Invitation

9.2. To Employees

Dear Employee:

The officers and directors of Kenworthy Corporation cordially invite you to a summer festival party at the South Pacific Clubhouse on Wednesday evening, July 21. This will be an informal get-together for all employees to show our appreciation for your hard work during this long, hot summer!

Cocktails will be served at 7 o'clock followed by a South Pacific smorgasbord at 8 o'clock. There will also be entertainment, fun, and relaxation for everyone until midnight.

We sincerely hope you can attend. Please send your reply to Jeanette Carson in the Business Office by July 15.

Cordially,

Although this is a general invitation to all employees, notice that it contains the same elements as a letter directed to a specific individual; it specifies the nature of the event, who is coming, where and when it is to be held, how long it will last, and the date by which a reply is needed. Model 9.2 is an invitation for employees only; sometimes spouses are also invited, and the first sentence of the letter would then be revised to indicate this.

Speaking Invitation

9.3. At Seminar

Dear Dr. Reisterhoff:

Members of the Society for the Evaluation of Human Issues have long admired your behavioral research activities and would enjoy learning more about your work. We would like to invite you to speak at the opening general session of our seminar on human issues to be held at the Bayside Motel, Atlantic City, New Jersey, on November 11, at 9 a.m. Since this session runs forty minutes, a twenty-five-minute address followed by a ten- to fifteen-minute question and answer period would be ideal.

About fifty people are expected to attend, most of them instructors, researchers, and other persons with backgrounds in the social and behavioral sciences and all of them concerned with the investigation of human issues. We are particularly interested in your findings pertaining to the effect of local opium production on the social-cultural populace of Burma. I know you recently filmed a documentary on this subject and could offer some valuable insights to our members.

In the hope that you will be able to join us, I'm enclosing a data form for you to complete; it will provide us with appropriate information to use in publicizing your appearance. Details concerning transportation and accommodations for speakers are included on the enclosed summary information sheet.

We do hope you can join us on November 11. I'd appreciate having your reply by September 15 so that we can finalize our program.

Sincerely,

The extent of information that should go into an invitation to speak depends on what type of accessory information sheets can be enclosed. If miscellaneous details can be sent by way of such enclosures, the letter can be kept relatively brief. Nevertheless, it should give basic facts—time, place, and so on—and request a reply by a specific date.

Membership Invitation

9.4. In Professional Society

Dear Ms. Jackson:

The Board of Directors of the Bateman Cultural Society cordially invites you to join the membership of this prestigious organization. As a Spanish instructor you would especially enjoy the many benefits available to participants, such as monthly meetings concerning international cultural and historical events and the exchange of ideas with colleagues who share your interests.

As the enclosed brochure explains, the Bateman Cultural Society is dedicated to the preservation and understanding of traditional cultural relationships throughout the world. The society's explorations through special projects and regular meetings are highly interesting and extremely valuable to all humankind.

We would welcome your membership and hope that you will take advantage of the enclosed application form so that your participation can begin immediately.

Cordially,

Clubs and associations often solicit memberships by letters of invitation. Usually, these letters are limited to describing general features of the organization, and more detail is provided by enclosing brochures and other material. Although the letter *invites* the prospect to join the organization, the membership usually has a price tag. Sometimes, in an effort to sound less like a sales letter, and when enclosed material clearly explains related charges, the invitation itself avoids mentioning fees.

Invitation to Support Charitable Organization

9.5. To Business Associate

Dear Paul:

As you know, I was recently appointed treasurer of the Winthrop Foundation. One of my new duties is to tell you and other interested persons something about this very worthwhile organization and invite your support during the coming year.

The Winthrop Foundation serves the greater Detroit area by providing emergency funds and work force during times of health-related crises. This aid might be anything from offering medical attention, supplies, and shelter to desperate flood, fire, or accident victims to setting up temporary hospital facilities when epidemics or other disease crises overload regular health-care establishments.

Time and again during the past twelve years of the foundation's existence it has demonstrated how much our metropolitan area needs this type of organization. But to survive, any charitable organization needs many contributions from people like you and me who one day may benefit from its life-saving assistance.

I hope you can see your way clear to support the foundation this year with a generous contribution. Anything you can give will be greatly appreciated and put to good use. Many thanks, Paul.

Best regards,

An *invitation* to support something is really a request to give something. Usually, the pattern is to begin with an invitation to support the cause or organization, followed by a synopsis of its features, and concluding with a request for a contribution.

Invitation to Special Event

9.6. An Open House

Dear Mrs. Hollingsworth:

The Board of Trustees of Marden Technological Institute cordially invite you to an open house on Thursday, April 9, to mark the opening of the Center for Advanced Studies. Since you have freely given so many hours of your time to fund-raising efforts for the new center, we sincerely hope you can join us on this happy occasion.

The center will be open from 10 a.m. until 5 p.m. on Thursday for visitors to view these magnificent facilities. Cocktails will be served in the Faculty Lounge from 5 until 7 p.m. for you and other special friends of the Institute.

We're all looking forward to seeing you again, Mrs. Hollingsworth. Please do let me know if you can join us for cocktails at the conclusion of visiting hours.

Cordially,

Facts given in an invitation such as model 9.6 might vary slightly depending on the recipient. For example, no address for the center is given since the recipient obviously is very familiar with its location. Nevertheless, this letter, like all invitations, must in all other respects be specific in details of time, place, nature of the event, who is coming, and so on.

REPLYING TO INFORMAL INVITATIONS

Courtesy demands that one respond promptly to an invitation. When time permits, the reply should always be in writing.

1. Repeat the essential details of time, date, and place.

2. Express pleasure when accepting an invitation.

3. Express regret and give a reason when declining an invitation.

Models 9.7 through 9.12 illustrate examples of several types of acceptance and several types of refusals of invitations by letter.

Accepting Invitation to Speak

9.7. At Club Dinner Meeting

Dear Mr. Santos:

It will be a pleasure to speak at the Retailers Club dinner meeting at the Holiday Inn on Friday, May 19, at 8 p.m.

I'll be glad to focus on the subject of the effect of large chain stores on small business development in the Southeast. As you suggested, I'll limit my address to thirty minutes.

Your invitation is most welcome, and I'm looking forward to meeting you and your colleagues in the Retailers Club.

Cordially,

Acceptances of speaking engagements should repeat the essential details—time, place, topic, and so on. When the invitation requests biographical data and a photograph, state in your acceptance letter that these items are enclosed or will be sent later. When an acceptance must be qualified, for example, based on a change in the suggested topic, give an explanation and, if appropriate, recommend an alternative.

Accepting Invitation to Lunch

9.8. With Colleague

Dear Natalie:

Yes, I certainly am free on the 14th to meet you for lunch at the
Red Lantern. Many thanks for asking. I'll look forward to seeing you
at 12 noon in the Jungle Lounge.

Regards,

As you can see from model 9.8, an acceptance of an invitation
to lunch can be brief. However, it should (1) display enthusiasm
and appreciation for the invitation and (2) repeat the essential details.

Accepting Invitation to Membership

9.9. On Special Committee

Dear Mr. Barker:

Thanks very much for the invitation to serve on the Harvest Club's
Education Committee. I appreciate the opportunity to participate
and will be glad to accept a position on the committee.

I'll look forward to receiving further information about my duties
and details about the next meeting.

Cordially,

The invitation being accepted in model 9.9 was really to work
on a volunteer basis. Nevertheless, as you can see, when something
is presented as an invitation, the reply of acceptance or declination
must show appreciation.

Refusing Invitation to Speak

9.10. At Conference

Dear Mr. Kittering:

I'm so sorry that I can't accept your thoughtful invitation to speak
at the Annual Crafts Conference in Seattle on August 8. My schedule calls for me to lecture in Houston most of that week.

Perhaps you would like to consider Professor George Parks from Row-
land Art Institute. He is well qualified to address your prospective

crafts audience and, if he will be free then, would no doubt be delighted to participate.

I very much regret that I can't join you in Seattle but do appreciate your thinking of me. Thanks very much.

Sincerely,

The refusal to an invitation to speak should express pleasure at being asked and regret at having to decline, giving a reason for the declination. If possible, the letter of refusal should suggest another speaker.

Refusing Invitation to Party

9.11. For Employees

Dear Mr. Hartley:

Much to my regret, a previous engagement on March 24 will prevent me from attending the Business Department's party for members of the staff and their friends.

Thank you anyway. I very much appreciated the invitation.

Sincerely,

The declination of an invitation to a party (or other social-business event) can either specify exactly why the invitation is being refused (perhaps you will be visiting someone out of town) or merely indicate that you have a previous engagement without saying what it is.

Refusing Invitation After Initial Acceptance

9.12. For Lunch

Dear Margaret:

I'm very sorry to let you know that an unexpected complication in my schedule has arisen, and I'll be unable to join you for lunch on September 5 as I had planned. Some important customers suddenly decided to pay us a visit, and I've been assigned the task of ushering them around on September 5 and 6.

I did so appreciate your invitation, Margaret, and am very disappointed that we won't have a chance to visit on the 5th. Let's hope that we can get together after my schedule clears up a little.

Best wishes,

The refusal of an invitation after first accepting it is similar to the initial declination: Express pleasure at being asked and regret at having to decline and give a reason for the refusal. A sentence can also be added, as illustrated in model 9.12, expressing hope to see the friend or associate later. The remark, however, should not obligate the person sending the invitation to extend another one later. If the writer wants to accept an invitation after first refusing it, the letter should state that the writer is happy to let the recipient know that he or she will be free after all and can join the person for lunch if the date and time are still convenient.

WRITING LETTERS FOR SPECIAL OCCASIONS

In addition to informal invitations, social-business correspondence involves many letters for special occasions—birthdays, anniversaries, holidays, illness, death, and many other similar events. Like all social-business letters, the letters for special occasions help build effective human relations among individuals and good public relations for your company.

1. Write naturally and sincerely.
2. Indicate the reason for your letter.
3. Focus your remarks on the recipient and the occasion and do not detract from it with other discussion.

Models 9.13 through 9.21 are examples of the many occasions that are acknowledged in social-business writing.

Birthday Wishes

9.13. To Business Associate

Dear Steve:

According to my calendar, November 16 is a red-letter day--yours!
This is to wish you the happiest birthday celebration ever.

All the best, Steve, on November 16 and on every day that follows for many years to come.

Regards,

Birthday wishes vary greatly depending on how well you know the person, how old the person is, whether or not age can be mentioned, and so on. Model 9.13 is appropriate for many instances since the tone is warm and friendly; yet it avoids remarking on the person's age and does not make overly familiar comments that some people might feel are too personal.

Expression of Sympathy: Individual

9.14. On Death of Spouse

Dear Jonathan:

Mrs. Wilson and I were deeply saddened by the death of your wife, Janet. We both enjoyed and respected her friendship and will miss her very much.

Our heartfelt sympathy goes out to you and your family. Do let me know if there's any way I can be of assistance in the weeks ahead.

Sincerely,

Sympathy letters will vary slightly, depending on your relationship with the recipient and his or her spouse. If you did not know the deceased very well, you might change the second sentence to "We know that everyone enjoyed and respected her and will miss her very much." In either case, the letter should avoid a macabre or flowery tone.

Expression of Sympathy: Company

9.15. On Death of Official

Dear Lou:

I was shocked to learn of Marshall McKay's untimely death yesterday. I know this will be a serious loss for you and many others at the Berkshire Corporation from both a personal and business standpoint.

My sincerest sympathy to you and your associates.

Regards,

Like the letter of sympathy to an individual, the letter concerning the death of a company executive must be brief and avoid excessive sentimentality. Unlike the letter to an individual upon loss of spouse or close friend, the company letter may omit the offer of assistance.

Letter to Accompany Gift

9.16. For Associate's Anniversary

Dear Madge:

Here's a little gift for you to help you celebrate your tenth anniversary at Norton Finance Company. Considering your solid record of progress and achievement and the many friends you've made during these ten years, I know this is a significant and happy occasion for you.

Very best wishes, Madge, for continued success and satisfaction in your career.

Cordially,

Letters to accompany gifts must briefly indicate that a gift is enclosed and explain the reason for the present. Any further comments should focus on the recipient and the cause for celebration--not on the gift. (In some companies, policy may prohibit sending or accepting a gift.)

Good Wishes, with Request for Favor

9.17. To Department Head

Dear Carl:

I just saw some of your new textured papers, and I think they're superb. Somehow you always manage to find the latest thing on the market, and your selections are always a huge success.

This new textured series is the most exciting yet, and I was wondering if you could make up a small swatch book for us to keep in the public relations office. It would help us greatly to have the samples available as we're talking with customers. If this isn't too much trouble, I'd certainly appreciate it.

Keep us posted on your amazing discoveries, Carl, and best of luck with the new series.

Cordially,

Sometimes it is possible to combine expressions of good luck with requests for something, such as model 9.17 illustrates. This practice, however, should be limited to situations in which the request will not overshadow the expression of good wishes. Preferably, begin and close the letter with flattering remarks and keep the request in a middle paragraph.

Thank You for Good Wishes

9.18. To Assistant

Dear Abe:

I really appreciated your complimentary remarks and good wishes on my promotion. Thanks so much.

Yes, I'll be glad to consider you for the Sherman account now that my new duties permit me to make such assignments. I'll contact you about this just as soon as I've had a chance to review the status of this account.

Best regards,

Although it is not appropriate to ask for a favor in a letter of congratulations, when you receive such a request, the only thing to do is to respond with a combination thank you and acknowledgment of the request. Your reply might grant the favor, refuse it (see 9.19), or agree to think about it and decide later.

Thank You for Good Wishes, Refusing Favor

9.19. To Assistant

Dear Mary:

Thanks ever so much for your thoughtful letter. I'll certainly take your good wishes with me when I join our midwestern field staff next month.

It was very flattering to learn that you would like to transfer with me. Knowing your fine capabilities so well, I wish this were possible. Unfortunately, there just aren't any administrative assistant openings in the Midwest at present. However, you might alert our personnel office here that you would like to transfer should a suitable opening occur later.

When the time comes, if you're still interested, I'll be most happy to recommend you for a transfer. Just let me know, Mary.

Best wishes,

Like any letter of refusal, the combination thank you and refusal letter should be considerate. To the extent possible it should have a positive tone even though it says no. It should give a reason for the refusal and, when practical, suggest other action to the recipient.

Thank You for Good Wishes, No Strings

9.20. Birthday Greetings Received

Dear Carroll:

How nice of you to remember my birthday. Your warm wishes will make my day much more enjoyable; in fact, I think I'll take your advice and celebrate in style!
Many thanks, Carroll.

Regards,

The simple thank you letter can be very brief. The important thing is to indicate genuine appreciation for the good wishes received.

Thank You for Special Kindness

9.21. During Family Illness

Dear Bob:

I want to thank you for all your help during Ellen's recent illness. Although she's getting along fine now, there were times when it was touch and go, and it was essential that I be at the hospital and assume extra responsibilities in caring for the children.

Without your assistance at the office, I could never have managed to be away from work that much. I don't know how you did it. I'm sure it put an added strain on your own work load. Both Ellen and I are grateful for your unfailing support and kindness during this difficult time. I just hope some day I can be of help to you.
Sincerest thanks, Bob.

Cordially,

Any response to a special act of kindness must show sincere gratitude. Although the letter can be relatively brief, it should comment enough about the act of kindness to let the recipient know that his or her efforts were truly appreciated and worthwhile.

10

Complaints and Adjustments

HUMAN errors, misunderstandings, and miscellaneous business problems breed complaints and the need to make adjustments. Eventually, you may find yourself on different sides of this unavoidable facet of business correspondence, both making and receiving complaints and subsequent adjustments. If there is a bright side to this area of communication, it is that complaints and adjustments can be used to your advantage to discover and correct problems. Fortunately, most situations can be resolved to everyone's satisfaction if the entire process is approached positively, without anger or resentment.

You will likely write and sign routine complaints and adjustments (such as 10.1) and may draft letters your boss prefers to sign (such as 10.2). Occasionally, a particularly sensitive or unusual complaint or adjustment (such as 10.5) can best be written by your boss, although you may be asked to polish and refine it. Monitor the success rate of your complaint and adjustment letters, and keep the ones that are effective in your computer file for reference and later use. (See the Model Sector Guide for other models of complaints and adjustments throughout the book, such as 7.18. Some complaints and adjustments are also handled by memo. For such samples, see chapter 13.)

If a failure in business operations, production, or personnel performance affects you adversely and unfairly, a complaint is usually justified. Letters of complaint often deal with matters such as shipments (10.1 and 10.7), employee performance (10.2), company service (10.3), and company products (10.4). An especially common source of complaint is the billing error (10.8-10.11). All of these complaints will differ depending on the focus of each criticism (complaining about a late shipment is different from complaining about someone's performance) and the seriousness of the complaint. Nevertheless, there is a general pattern you can follow in most letters of complaint, as illustrated in models 10.1 through 10.11.

Handling adjustments requires tact and understanding. If someone is unhappy it is important to correct the situation or you might lose a customer or friend of the company, and the company's image could be damaged. Like letters of complaint, adjustment letters might involve almost anything from a claim for damage (10.13) to an explanation of unsatisfactory work (10.19), and the composition of adjustment letters will vary according to the type of adjustment being made and the seriousness of the problem. Models 10.12 through 10.21, however, illustrate a general pattern and tone to follow in writing your own adjustment letters.

MAKING COMPLAINTS

Some people complain at the slightest inconvenience; others never speak up even under the worst conditions. The best position to take is probably somewhere between those two extremes. The only way to be certain you are not moving too far in either direction is to avoid writing a hasty letter in anger and to take time to evaluate your justification in making a complaint.

1. State all details relative to the complaint.
2. Specify what type of adjustment you desire.
3. Be firm but do not display anger or an unreasonable attitude.
4. Be fair in your criticism and request for resolution.

The following eleven models are examples of the wide variety of complaints you may have to write in your office.

Incomplete Shipment

10.1. Of Stationery

Ladies and Gentlemen:

Our May 5 order for 10,000 company letterheads and matching envelopes has arrived incomplete. The correct number of letterheads was included with the shipment we received yesterday, but only 5,000 of the matching envelopes were delivered.

If the additional 5,000 envelopes are en route separately, please disregard this notice. If they are not, I'd appreciate your letting me know the anticipated delivery date right away. It's very important that we receive the rest of our order as soon as possible.

Thank you very much.

Sincerely,

Notification of a problem with a shipment should specify details such as delivery date, product in question, quantities ordered, and so on. If it is important to have the problem corrected quickly, this should be made clear. However, never ask someone to rush something to you when you really have no urgent need for it. This model illustrates the mildest form of complaint—little more than routine notification of an error or problem and a request for rectification.

Unsatisfactory Performance: Individual

10.2. Of Employee

Dear Ms. Jackson:

I would like to request a replacement for Lynda Belknap, the part-time computer operator sent to us last week from your agency. I'm sorry to let you know that her performance has been unsatisfactory.

We had indicated to you our need for someone with good word processing skills, but Ms. Belknap apparently has minimal word processing experience. Her speed is too slow, and the quality of her work is insufficient for our needs. Although in other respects--attitude, cooperativeness, and the like--we were satisfied, it is imperative that our assistants be fast and accurate word processors. We would therefore like to have a replacement ready to begin next Monday, the 14th.

I'd appreciate a telephone call from you in advance to discuss the qualifications of the new assistant so that we can avoid further problems. Thanks very much.

Sincerely,

It is likely that the writer of this complaint was more annoyed than the letter indicates. She restrained herself, however, (1) because she wanted further help from the agency and (2) she did not want to condemn the employee's performance excessively or unfairly. Nevertheless, the letter makes it clear that the situation is unacceptable and must be corrected. If the problem had been more serious, the writer might have insisted on some credit adjustment as well.

Unsatisfactory Service: Company

10.3. Late Deliveries

Dear Mr. MacAllen:

For several months we have been experiencing late deliveries from your company on parts for our hand-operated power tools. This unfortunate situation is causing many of our customers to question the prompt service and maintenance guarantee that is part of our sales policy.

Naturally, we are concerned about the increasing dissatisfaction among our customers and believe we must find a solution without delay. Therefore, I'd appreciate it if you would let me know immediately what can be done to correct this situation. I'm sure you will understand that if you are unable to provide deliveries on a reliable schedule, we will have no alternative but to seek another source for our power tool supplies and parts.

I'll look forward to hearing from you within the week, and I do hope you'll have a solution for this persistent problem of late deliveries. Thanks very much. I appreciate your cooperation.

Sincerely,

Model 10.3 is an example of a letter that basically lays it on the line: Correct the problem and do it now or we will go elsewhere for our parts. Notice, however, that the letter makes the point clearly without unrestrained anger, name calling, or excessive criticism. The writer wants results but does not want to insult or anger the recipient so much that he will be disinclined to make an effort to correct the problem. This is not the only alternative; under other circumstances the writer might have stated that he wants to end relations with the supplier and have all deliveries cease immediately.

Unsatisfactory Product

10.4. Defective Addressing Machine

Dear Mr. Baker:

I'm sorry to let you know that the model 1920 addressing machine installed last month is malfunctioning. We have followed all instructions very carefully, and your service representative has called twice to investigate the problem. But the equipment is apparently defective.

Please let us know when we can expect a replacement from you. Our next mailing is scheduled for August 9, and we will need properly functioning equipment installed by the first of the month to meet this deadline.

Thanks for your help and cooperation. I'll look forward to hearing from you shortly.

Sincerely,

There are several alternatives when a product is unsatisfactory: (1) ask for a replacement, (2) ask for further repairs, or (3) ask to return the equipment and receive a refund. Model 10.4 concerns a common response—the writer believes it is at least worth trying a replacement since there is nothing to lose by doing so.

Criticism of New System

10.5. To Department Head

Dear Ms. Vinson:

Your efforts to simplify and reorganize our billing procedures have been a welcome sign of long overdue reforms in this area. I've followed with interest the new system established by your department last month and would like to offer some comments for your consideration.

The new system allows for billing of all society members on a single anniversary date, once each year, with the usual second, third, and delinquent notices. Apparently, this confines the task of invoice preparation to a single month during which additional computer assistance can be easily acquired and supervised. No doubt this exclusive focus on the total billing function at one time encourages many efficiencies and an extra lever of control.

Unfortunately, the single billing date also discourages seasonal and periodic monetary returns. We now must hope all members are best able to pay in April or soon thereafter. If they are not, since there is no dispersion of collections, they will simply become delinquent members. It is no longer possible to increase renewals through use of regular monthly and seasonal payment periods. Moreover, our receivables are now heavy in the spring and weak at other times, even though our expenditures do not follow a similar pattern. In short, by solving a few problems such as the ease of hiring temporary help only once a year, we may have introduced more serious problems pertaining to cash flow and year-round payment potential.

Possibly, we should have another look at the new system, and I'd like to have your thoughts on this matter. Why don't you let me know when you have some ideas pulled together, and we can get together for lunch to discuss the matter further. I'll look forward to hearing from you soon, Ms. Vinson. Thanks very much.

Cordially,

Criticism is most effective when it is constructive. If it alienates or offends the recipient it will probably be ineffective. Therefore, model 10.5 opens with a word of praise. Next, the criticism that follows is supported with specific detailed facts and suggestions. Finally, the letter closes courteously and in a friendly tone recommends lunch and more discussion.

Misrepresentation

10.6. Of Product

Dear Mr. Scott:

For several days we have been monitoring a serious problem concerning the six New Lite 200 ceiling fans that one of your clerks sold us on July 27.

Our reason for ordering the fans was to replace older fans that were the source of numerous complaints from our staff because of their excessive noise. Your clerk had analyzed our problem and had recommended the New Lite 200 as the quietest fan available for our needs. Unfortunately, he did not tell us that the New Lite 200 operates quietly only on a slow (low) setting. Since our rooms are quiet large, as we had indicated when discussing the matter with your clerk, we must use a medium or higher speed. When the fans arrived, we discovered that at those speeds, the fans are just as noisy as the older ones we had replaced.

The new fans clearly are not performing quietly as we were assured they would do. Therefore, they are of no use to us, and we are asking that you immediately exchange the New Lite fans for six Bernmore 601 fans, applying the full purchase price of the New Lites to the Bernmores. We also ask that you arrange for the immediate rewiring of the six fans at no cost to us.

Please telephone me at 601-4149 to let me know when we may expect your service representative to install the Bernmores.

Sincerely,

When a product or service has been misrepresented, you are entitled to an adjustment. Most people would ask to have a full refund or to exchange the product or service for something else. Although excessive hostility in a letter is always inadvisable, a complaint concerning misrepresentation should nevertheless firmly state that the situation is unacceptable and that a prompt adjustment is expected. The tone of the letter might be softer or sharper than that in model 10.6 depending on your relationship with the supplier and the supplier's reputation for handling adjustments fairly.

Omission of Enclosures

10.7. Vital Data Missing

Dear Mr. Kirby:

As I explained by telephone this morning, your shipment of forty data-processing manuals (Data Processing Today, Ramon, 0073621, $8.98 ea.) arrived just in time for the opening class at our Central Training Center. However, we were disappointed to discover that the supplementary instructor's guide and answer key was missing.

Since classes have already started, we are urgently in need of this supplementary instructor's material. The course lasts only four weeks, so you can see that the material will be of little use unless it reaches us without further delay. Therefore, I'd appreciate it if you would send this material immediately by overnight express.

Thanks very much for your help.

Sincerely,

The writer in model 10.7 obviously has a problem. Class has started and he is already using the textbooks that arrived. Since it is too late to cancel the entire order and look elsewhere for suitable material, he has little alternative but to pressure the supplier to get the missing supplementary aids to him as soon as possible. Thus an urgent telephone call to the supplier is followed with a letter repeating the details of the problem.

Billing Error: Merchandise

10.8. Goods Not Ordered

Ladies and Gentlemen:

We have just received your June 30 invoice no. 06400 for $84.88 for one dozen no. 221 Hunt printer ribbons. Our records show that one dozen ribbons were ordered from you and received in April. However, they were paid by our check no. 713 for $84.88 on May 15.

Therefore, invoice no. 06400 was apparently sent in error, and I'm returning it with this letter.

Sincerely,

It is not unusual to be billed twice for the same purchase or to be billed for someone else's purchase or just to be billed for something neither you nor anyone else ordered. Unless this error is repeated, though, a harsh or stern complaint is not justified. Therefore, simply return the invoice and explain carefully why you should not have been billed.

Billing Error: Amount

10.9. Overcharged for Purchase

Ladies and Gentlemen:

We have just received your August 17 invoice no. B1-2992 for $170.69 for one black, three-drawer, Masterlock file cabinet. According to the sales slip presented to us at the time of purchase, the total price should be $159.70.

Therefore, we are returning your invoice no. B1-2992. If you will issue a corrected invoice, we will be happy to send you our payment promptly upon receipt of it.

Sincerely,

Model 10.9, representing another type of billing error, is similar to model 10.8. Notice that in each case the incorrect invoice was returned to the sender.

Billing Error: Credit Card

10.10 Returned Purchase Not Credited

Ladies and Gentlemen:

Account 12-343-001, Regina M. Edwards, Brock Hardware

Your April 1 statement to Ms. Edwards shows a charge of $87 for a Pointmore security light. However, the product was returned to you on March 4, and I am enclosing a copy of the credit slip.

I'd appreciate it if you would send me a corrected statement showing that Ms. Edwards' account has been credited for the full amount of the returned security light.

Thank you.

Sincerely,

Billing errors pertaining to charge accounts are handled much the same as errors related to other types of purchases. It is helpful, however, to begin the letter with a subject line that states the account number, the account holder, and his or her company's name.

Billing Error: Computer

10.11. Persistent Error

Dear Ms. Parsons:

On July 1 we received our fifth bill from your store for $124 for a model 86 electronic calculator. The other four invoices (March 1, April 1, May 1, and June 1) were promptly returned to your credit department with a letter repeating each time that we have never leased, purchased, or even seen a model 86 calculator. Although we once maintained an account with you, it was canceled a year ago when our offices were moved to another location. Since then we have made no purchases of any sort from you either on account or by cash. However, your latest invoice was accompanied by a letter stating that the machine, which we do not have, will be reclaimed if we do not make immediate payment.

Since our previous letters were apparently ignored and since your computer seems determined to perpetuate this situation, I'd appreciate it if you would personally locate the error and have it corrected immediately.

Thank you for your help.

Sincerely,

When a billing error becomes persistent, it is time to bypass the computer and get in touch with someone who is likely to be in a position to help you. This means that you should address your letter to a specific individual, or if you cannot find a name, use a title such as manager, customer relations; manager, billing department; or manager, credit department. Although you may be furious if the problem has been persistent, keep the tone of your letter firm but cool and calm enough to get some positive results. Angry threats and wild statements might cause someone to classify your letter as that of a crank, and it could then end up in a wastebasket.

HANDLING ADJUSTMENTS

It is always advisable to handle matters of adjustments promptly, whether your letter grants an adjustment, refuses to make one, or just offers an explanation for something.

1. Be considerate and understanding in your letter.
2. If you are at fault, apologize and try to rectify the situation.
3. Do not allow your explanations to sound like justifications for a fault.

Like complaints, adjustments can vary greatly. Models 10.12 through 10.21 are examples of the major types of adjustment letters: requests for adjustment, letters of explanation, and letters granting or refusing an adjustment request.

Requesting a Refund

10.12. Merchandise Returned

Ladies and Gentlemen:

I am returning for a refund one six-ounce jar of Magic Miracle Lotion, which I purchased on July 6 by check for $16.95. Your catalog description states that if a customer is not fully satisfied, the unused portion of the lotion may be returned and a full refund will be sent promptly. After one week's use, I am convinced the lotion is ineffective and want to take advantage of your money-back guarantee.

Please make the refund check payable to Lois J. Harrington and send it to 903 Mockingbird Lane, Princeton, NJ 08540.

Thank you very much.

Sincerely,

A request for a refund should describe the object enclosed, list its price, indicate how it was paid for, and specify where the refund should be sent. If a special return policy is involved, the letter should also make reference to this.

Claim for Damage

10.13. Merchandise Broken

Ladies and Gentlemen:

Upon unpacking the framed print delivered to me on November 4 by Arcane Truck Delivery Service, I found that the glass over the picture had been cracked in transit, with one sharp edge piercing the print beneath.

Since the package was insured by the mailer, Novis Art Gallery, Concord, Massachusetts, I would appreciate having your claims adjuster call as soon as possible to inspect the damaged merchandise. If you have a claims form I should complete in the meantime, please send it to me at the address shown on this letterhead.

Thank you very much.

Sincerely,

Model 10.13 concerns a claim to be filed with the transporting company. Other claims might be registered with the sender, with the U.S. Postal Service, or with some other agency. In most cases a form must be filled out; sometimes an adjuster must call to inspect the damage or you must take the merchandise to the adjuster's office. In all cases, act promptly and notify the appropriate person immediately upon discovering the damage.

Request for Discount

10.14. On Delayed Shipment

Dear Mr. Bradley:

Your representative informed me today that the sales brochures we ordered on May 7 are almost ready but will not reach us by the deadline we had agreed upon. These brochures were intended in part for distribution at our annual conference and in part for a mail campaign to sell the books and journals advertised in them.

Because we will not have the material to distribute at our conference, we will experience a substantial loss in book sales; usually, we sell about 500 copies at these events when appropriate sales literature is available. In view of this problem, and since you failed to meet the deadlines specified with our order, I trust you will provide a satisfactory discount on the order as partial compensation for the loss this delay will cause. A reduction of 40 percent of your charges would be appropriate since that is the percentage of brochures we had intended to use at the conference.

I'd appreciate receiving your confirmation of this proposed settlement as soon as possible. Thank you.

Sincerely,

To justify a request for a discount based on a delayed shipment,
you must (1) indicate that an earlier delivery date was guaranteed
and (2) show how you will definitely suffer a loss because of the
supplier's failure to meet the agreed-upon deadline. You can also
specify a desired discount, although the eventual settlement may
well be less than the amount requested. As long as your facts are
accurate, the type of complaint illustrated in model 10.14 is completely
justified.

Granting Adjustment: Billing

10.15. Error Corrected

Dear Mrs. Swanson:

We are enclosing a corrected invoice for the linens sent to you on
December 2. The price of $64.50 has been changed to $46.50.

Please accept our sincere apologies for this clerical error and any
inconvenience it has caused you. We very much appreciate your interest in our merchandise and hope we will have an opportunity to
serve you again.

Cordially,

When granting an adjustment for an error made by your company,
state the correction details—item purchased, erroneous charge, corrected charge, and so on—and extend a sincere apology for the
error and any inconvenience it has caused the customer. If further
sales might be possible, you might close with some indication that
you hope to be of service again.

Granting Adjustment: Damage Claim

10.16. Merchandise Replaced

Dear Mr. Willis:

We were very sorry to learn that the portable vacuum you recently
ordered arrived with a cracked hull. Thank you for returning the
damaged product so promptly.

A replacement model of the same style, size, color, and price is enclosed. It has been carefully inspected before packing to insure that you will not be troubled again with a similar problem.

We sincerely regret the delay and the inconvenience this has caused you but hope you will now be pleased with your new vacuum.

Thank you for your patience.

Cordially,

The response to a damage claim is determined by the customer's request and the company's policy. Many companies ask the customer to return the product and then offer him or her a choice of a replacement, a refund, or credit on a later purchase. In model 10.16 the customer had returned the product and had requested a replacement product. Similar to all adjustments responding to a justifiable complaint, this model offers an apology for the problem and any inconvenience it has caused.

Explanation for Delayed Shipment

10.17. Supplies Overdue

Dear Ms. Cramer:

We are very sorry that our shipment of frame kits to you has been delayed. The factory that manufactures the unfinished frames sent to us for finishing had experienced some problems in filling our orders last month. We received a new supply of frames on Tuesday, however, and expect to finish them immediately and ship your kits on May 24.

We sincerely regret any inconvenience this has caused you and hope your order will soon be filled to your satisfaction.

Thank you so much for your patience.

Cordially,

Customers are entitled to an explanation of overdue orders. One thing to guard against in such letters is a tendency to make weak excuses sound like a justification for the delay. Before you compose the letter, decide what the facts are and state them briefly and accurately. If there is no good reason for the delay, do not invent one or try to dress up a poor one, but simply apologize and indicate when the order will be filled.

Explanation of Oversight

10.18. A Missing Part

Dear Mr. Shaw:

We're very sorry that your humidifier was delivered with the roto-belt missing. A new belt is enclosed for you now.

Roto-belts are shipped to us separately, and they are supposed to be fitted on the humidifiers as soon as they are unpacked. Apparently, someone accidentally overlooked the unit that by chance was delivered to you.

Please accept our sincere apologies for this oversight and any inconvenience it may have caused you. We appreciate your interest in our humidifiers and hope yours will contribute to many years of your comfort and good health.

Cordially,

The letter explaining an oversight is similar to other adjustment letters such as models 10.16 and 10.17. Letters are not always sent in these cases, but a thoughtful explanation is a good way to improve customer relations.

Explanation of Unsatisfactory Work

10.19. Poor Printing Quality

Dear Ms. Clark:

You are absolutely right--the quality of printing on your November issue of Executive Newsletter is below our usual standards. Although I believe it meets the minimum standards of the trade, I agree completely that the printing can and should be improved on future issues.

My press operator tells me that the press used for 11- by 17-inch work was performing poorly the week your newsletter was run. Since then, we've had the service representative look at the machine, and the problem has been corrected. You may be certain that our production supervisor will monitor the press runs more closely hereafter so that this problem will never occur again.

We appreciate your concern and are very sorry that you were unhappy with the job. Please accept our sincere apologies. We value your business and are going to do our utmost to provide high-quality work for you at all times.

Sincerely,

Follow a basic rule when you have to explain unsatisfactory work: When you are wrong, admit it and apologize. The customer is likely to be irritated in such a situation and will not tolerate feeble excuses or a rationale for low-quality work. In addition to giving an explanation, stress your intent to avoid such problems in the future and your sincere desire to satisfy the customer.

Refusing Adjustment on Late Delivery

10.20. Of Merchandise

Dear Mrs. Pendleton:

We were very sorry to learn that your order for two dozen crystal goblets arrived after your reception for Senator Juliet. Unfortunately, our store has no policy providing for a reduction in cost of merchandise under these circumstances.

However, if the crystal has not been used, it can be returned for a full refund or for credit toward another purchase. Should you decide upon one of these alternatives, simply return the unused crystal to the customer service desk at our Madison Avenue Store where it was purchased and specify your choice of credit or refund.

We sincerely regret any inconvenience you have experienced and hope we'll have an opportunity to serve you again.

Cordially,

A letter refusing to make an adjustment should be especially tactful and considerate. Avoid a blunt, abrupt no. Model 10.20 offers two alternatives to the customer's request for a discount: a full refund or credit toward another purchase. Any refusal letter will seem less harsh if other alternatives or suggestions are offered so that the customer does not feel it is all a total loss.

Refusing to Grant a Refund

10.21. On Sale Merchandise

Dear Mr. Rhoades:

We were very sorry to learn that you were not satisfied with the cassettes purchased during our spring sale last month. However, our store does not allow for returns or refunds on sale merchandise.

Although we cannot offer a refund on the sale cassettes, we do have a full line of other cassettes, as well as CDs, at regular price; any of them could be returned unused and unopened if you later decided against them.

We very much regret that you are unhappy with your purchase and hope your next selections will be much more satisfactory.

Cordially,

Model 10.21 is similar to model 10.20 in that the tone is sympathetic, even though the letter is saying no. Also, this model makes a suggestion so that the customer will know a sincere effort is being made to help him in spite of the policy that prevents him from receiving the refund he wants.

11

Credit and Collection

BUSINESS writers often stress that we live in a credit society or an age of credit. It's true that matters of credit and collection affect nearly every type of organization, large or small. Thus it is important in the modern business office to be familiar with the types of correspondence generated in credit and collection activities, whether your own office handles these matters, whether your company has a credit department for this purpose, or whether you use an outside collection agency.

Although financial matters are usually sensitive, many of the letters pertaining to credit and collection are routine requests and responses. You may write these letters (such as 11.4) and mail them under your own signature, or you may compose the letters for your boss's signature (such as 11.5). When communications reach a serious level (see 11.11), your boss may prefer to draft the basic letter, although you may be expected to refine and polish it. No matter who signs the letter, however, most credit and collection correspondence follows a very definite pattern that you can use in composing your own messages; many credit and collection situations, in fact, are so routine that they are handled by forms and form letters (see 15.8 and 15.9). The letters, therefore, should be stored in your computer file for recall and use in future situations. (The Model Selector Guide will lead you to other credit and collection models throughout the book, such as 6.12 in chapter 6.)

Credit letters deal with the financial status of a person or company—someone's ability to pay or someone's history of meeting his or her obligations. Both individuals and businesses are concerned about their financial reputations, and this concern must be carefully considered and respected when composing credit letters. Credit correspondence typically involves requests for credit or credit information (11.1-11.3 and 11.5-11.7) and responses to those requests (11.4 and 11.8-11.12).

The way that you handle your collection correspondence depends on the size of your company and the number of situations you must handle. The most familiar approach to the problem of overdue accounts is the collection-letter series (11.13-11.18). This series provides examples of major steps in collection proceedings, from the casual reminder to the final, last-resort prelude to legal action.

WRITING CREDIT LETTERS

In one respect credit letters are goodwill letters because they concern the relationship—past, present, and future—between two parties. This immediately suggests that the credit letter must try to preserve or establish a satisfactory relationship while still accomplishing its financial purpose.

1. When requesting credit, assuming the request is realistic, provide all information the recipient will need to process the request.

2. When responding to credit requests, be completely honest and accurate but also be considerate of the writer's feelings and needs.

Models 11.1 through 11.12 provide examples of the major types of credit letters: requesting credit or credit information, supplying credit information, and responding to requests for credit.

Request for Credit: Individual

11.1. To Department Store

Ladies and Gentlemen:

I would like to open a charge account at Baker's Department Store. Please send a credit application to me at 1440 Newbury Street, Charlotte, VT 05445.

Thank you.

Sincerely,

This model illustrates the simplest form of credit request. Most organizations have their own credit applications that must be completed. So the letter of request for credit does not provide any facts but merely asks for the application, which is then completed and returned to the store.

Request for Credit: Business

11.2. To Supplier

Dear Mr. Adams:

The Wahlgreen Construction Company is continually in need of quality paint and home building supplies at attractive prices. We are familiar with your fine products and would like to place some orders with you in the coming months.

Would you be able to provide your usual credit terms to us for quantity purchases? I'm enclosing the name of our bank and three suppliers with whom we have done business in the past. Please let me know if you will need further information for us to open an account with you.

Thanks very much for your consideration, Mr. Adams. We look forward to an opportunity to use your supplies in many of our future construction jobs.

Sincerely,

A business can seek credit on purchases in a number of ways. You might get letters of recommendation from other credit sources before asking a new supplier for terms. Or you might simply ask for an application, using much the same approach as in model 11.1. The example shown here illustrates a third and common procedure—writing to ask for credit, indicating that purchases will be forthcoming, and enclosing the names of credit references instead of the actual letters. Model 11.2 also indicates that further information will be provided if needed.

Request for Credit Information

11.3. About New Business

Dear Mr. Brewster:

Middle River Sporting Goods has just sent us a large order with a request to make this and future purchases on account. The manager, William Wright, gave your company's name as a credit reference.

Since Middle River is a new store, your experience with them may be limited. However, I'd appreciate having your evaluation of their potential and your recommendations regarding an extension of credit. Your comments will be kept strictly confidential.

Thanks very much, Mr. Brewster. I appreciate your help and cooperation.

Cordially,

Requests for credit information about businesses are similar, whether the business is new or well established. Assuming a standard form is not sent for the recipient to fill out, the letter usually asks the reference source to comment on his or her experience concerning the applicant's performance in previous credit situations. The reference source should be assured that all remarks will be held in the strictest confidence. Also, any letter of request must conclude with an expression of appreciation.

Providing Credit Information

11.4. About Customer

Dear Mr. Gibbs:

Our experience with Whitcomb Industries has been excellent. According to our credit department, they have faithfully paid our invoices within thirty days throughout the nearly three years of our association. Most of their purchases have ranged between $2,000 and $4,000 a month.

Based on our own satisfaction with this account, I believe you could justifiably consider extending a similar amount of credit to Whitcomb Industries.

Let me know if there's anything else I can do to help. Best regards.

Cordially,

One of the most important requirements in providing credit information is accuracy. You should not make decisions for others, but your facts should be clear and reliable, whether they are complimentary or negative. Model 11.4 comments on a good customer. Notice, however, that even this letter carefully states that the recipient *might* (not should) consider extending a similar, but not unlimited, amount of credit.

Inviting New Account: Business

11.5. For Office Supply Store

Dear Ms. Ringley:

We would like to make it easier for you to keep your office well supplied with the myriad of materials you need every day, from paper clips to sophisticated business forms. Therefore, we have opened an account for you in the name of your company; your credit is good at Carson's Office Supply, and no application is necessary.

Our accounts for preferred customers such as your company are based on a thirty-day billing cycle (2%, 10 days). Throughout each month you may make as many purchases of any size as you wish, with no minimum number required at any time. Whether you telephone, write, or visit our store, all you need to do is give us your order and your name. Incidentally, we provide free, same-day delivery service for local customers.

We hope you'll enjoy the convenience of having an account at Carson's. I know we'll enjoy having you as a customer and look forward to hearing from you soon.

Cordially,

It is common practice for some establishments to add new customers by offering credit before they even ask for it. The letter inviting such business should provide details concerning the terms, the billing cycle, whether an application must be completed later, and so on. It is important to avoid alarming the prospective customer with any suggestion of obligation on the customer's part. If there are benefits that accompany the account, such as free delivery service, they should be mentioned as well.

Inviting New Account: Individual

11.6. For Clothing Store

Dear Mrs. Lewis:

Did you know that Porter's Department Store has just expanded its line of household products to include lawn and garden tools and outdoor furniture? Actually, we have increased the number of products in all our departments during the past few months to make Porter's the most complete clothing and home service center in your area.

I thought you might like to know that in just another month, on August 20, our fall clothing sales will begin. So that you can take advantage of the great savings that will be offered on men's, women's, and children's wear, I'm enclosing one of our charge-card applications. As you can see, it's very brief and will take only a minute to complete. If you mail it to us or leave it at our credit office within the next few days, we will be able to process it and, upon approval, send you your new charge plate in time for use during our big August sale days. Just check on the application whether you prefer our thirty-day, full-payment plan or a revolving account that offers low monthly payments on all purchases up to $300.

Why not take a minute right now to complete your application. A charge account at Porter's will make your shopping so much easier and enjoyable. We hope to hear from you soon.

Sincerely,

Model 11.6 represents another example of seeking new customers by offering credit before the prospective customer asks for it. In this case, however, the prospect is asked to complete an application, so credit is *not* guaranteed in the initial letter.

Activating Old Account

11.7. At Service Establishment

Dear Mr. Greenburg:

We haven't seen you since last October and are wondering if our service was not completely satisfactory. If anything displeased you, I'd appreciate knowing about it so that we can make amends without delay. Just call me at 224-3000, and I'll take care of the matter at once.

It was always a pleasure to see you at Mike's Foreign Car Service, and if your car is due for servicing soon, I'd like to offer you a 15 percent discount for this work as a special welcome-back gift. Incidentally, we have a new supply of foreign car accessories on hand now and throughout this month are selling all discontinued items at a 10 to 30 percent reduction. We'll be glad to put whatever you select on your account: Even though we haven't seen you recently, your credit is still good at Mike's.

Come in soon, and I personally guarantee we will do our best to insure that you are completely satisfied from this day on.

Cordially,

Letters reactivating old accounts will vary, depending on how long the customer has been gone, why he probably left, and so on. Model 11.7 is typical in that it (1) adopts a thoughtful tone and (2) offers an enticement—discounts.

Refusing Credit: With Alternative

11.8. To Company

Dear Mr. Brooks:

We appreciated your interest in our new plastic storage containers and want to thank you for inquiring about credit.

As much as we would like to extend credit to your firm, an investigation of the references you supplied indicates there were occasional problems in making periodic payments on schedule. It is our policy in such cases to ship merchandise only C.O.D. or after advance cash payment. Perhaps you would like to place orders now on this basis and apply for credit privileges again in another six months.

Thanks very much for thinking of us. I hope we'll have an opportunity to provide the storage containers you need.

Sincerely,

A letter of refusal should always be as thoughtful as possible. In model 11.8, the writer does not want to lose a prospective customer and thus recommends cash orders now and a reapplication for credit later.

Refusing Credit: Without Alternative

11.9. To Individual

Dear Mrs. Samuels:

Thank you for your recent application for a charge account at The Gift Shoppe. It was a pleasure to learn about your interest in our gifts.

As much as we would like to open an account for you, the credit information we received indicates that you have experienced serious difficulties in making payments on your other accounts. Unfortunately, our policy prevents us from opening accounts under these circumstances.

Meanwhile, we hope that you will take advantage of the many exciting gift selections in our store available on a cash basis.

Sincerely,

When credit information points to a consistently poor credit risk, there is no point in suggesting that the applicant reapply soon again. In this model, the writer does not even mention sending merchandise C.O.D. He does, however, close with a routine suggestion that the customer shop on a cash basis. Notice that the letter adopts a relatively gentle tone, even though the writer doubtless is unimpressed with the applicant's record.

Refusing Special Credit Terms

11.10. Quantity Discount

Dear Mrs. McDaniel:

We were happy to learn that you are considering our detachable countertops for your lakeside cottages. They are, indeed, popular in motels, cottages, and other resort accommodations that have a combined living-kitchen area. I'm sorry, though, that we have no provision for quantity discounts on orders in the range of 25 to 30 units. It would be necessary for us to order above 100 units from the factory to receive a markdown that we could pass along to our customers.

I do hope this won't discourage you from selecting our countertops for your cottages. We can guarantee that they are not only attractive but are also highly durable and thus well suited for heavy tourist usage. We believe the price of $59.95 per unit, including installation, is very reasonable in itself and that it would be hard to find a better value anywhere.

Let us know if we can take your order now so that we can make certain the countertops will be ready for installation before the June rush begins. I know you'll be delighted with them.

Sincerely,

When credit is refused for some reason unrelated to the applicant's record, every effort should be made to retain the customer's business. Model 11.10 illustrates a case in which there is nothing wrong with the customer's credit; the writer simply cannot offer a discount. Therefore, the letter says no but does a selling job in hopes of getting the order anyway.

Canceling Credit

11.11. Of Company

Dear Mr. Parks:

Much to my regret, I must inform you that we will have to stop extending credit to your company, effective immediately. As the enclosed statement of your account shows, your balance of $5,670.80 is long past due, and no payments have been made in the past ninety days.

We hope that a check for the overdue amount will be forthcoming in the next few days. In the meantime, though, I'm sure you will understand that we are unable to continue this outstanding indebtedness any further.

Sincerely,

Letter 11.11 should not be confused with a collection letter. The main purpose of this communication is simply to cancel the credit arrangement, even though the letter also asks the debtor to make payment. The assumption is that other correspondence has been and will be generated to collect the past-due account. In other cases, though, the writer might prefer to combine the letters, with cancellation and collection a joint objective in a single letter.

Settling Misunderstanding

11.12. Of Payment Plan

Dear Ms. Jacobs:

Thank you for returning our September 1 invoice no. 26170 for $212.90. You are absolutely right that you should be billed in installments for this charge.

Apparently, our billing department misunderstood my instructions. I have informed them that you are to be billed monthly at the rate of $20 plus a service charge of 1.5 percent on the unpaid balance. A corrected invoice will be sent to you shortly.

Please accept our apologies for this misunderstanding. We appreciate your calling it to our attention.

Sincerely,

When someone—buyer or seller—misunderstands payment matters, the problem should be straightened out immediately. If the customer has misunderstood, the situation should be explained carefully, but he or she should never be criticized for failing to understand the terms of a sale. If the seller has made a mistake, as is the case in model 11.12, it should be rectified promptly and an apology issued immediately.

PREPARING THE COLLECTION-LETTER SERIES

A single letter does not always result in collection of an overdue account. Knowing this, collection writers plan their correspondence with the assumption that they may have to write several letters, each one becoming more forceful than the one before. This program of collection correspondence is often called the collection-letter series.

1. Create a campaign of four to six letters, from a casual reminder to a prelude to legal action.
2. Gauge the tone of the letters from the beginning, with a friendly reminder, to the conclusion, with a final, strong plea preceding legal action.
3. Know the facts of the situation thoroughly before developing the content of any of the letters.
4. Always give the customer an opportunity to meet his or her obligation, no matter how late.

Models 11.13 through 11.18 represent a typical series of six collection letters. If fewer letters are desired, models 11.15, 11.16, and 11.17 (series nos. 3, 4, and 5) could be combined into one or possibly two letters. Although many writers employ humor in their letters, most collection letters are more straightforward, as this series illustrates.

Collection Letter 1

11.13. A Casual Reminder

Dear Mr. Lawrence:

Just a friendly reminder that your payment of $270.98 will be very much appreciated.

If your check is already in the mail, please disregard this notice and accept our thanks. If it is not, won't you take a moment to mail it today?

Cordially,

The first letter sent when an account becomes overdue is usually short and friendly. The letter often suggests that the check may already be in the mail, and the customer is told how much the payment will be appreciated.

Collection Letter 2

11.14. A Strong Reminder

Dear Mr. Lawrence:

Another thirty days have passed and your payment of $270.98 has not yet arrived.

Since we have not heard from you, we assume that the balance is correct and that your records agree with ours. Won't you therefore send us your check today or let us hear from you right away before this unpaid balance affects your credit standing?

Your cooperation will be very much appreciated, Mr. Lawrence. Thank you.

Sincerely,

Letter 2, often sent thirty days after letter 1, becomes more serious and uses stronger language. The customer is told that (1) the payment due must be correct since he has not questioned it and (2) he may lose his credit standing if he does not pay promptly or at least explain why he is not sending payment.

Collection Letter 3

11.15. The Discussion Letter

Dear Mr. Lawrence:

We were disappointed that we did not hear from you in response to our last letter concerning your overdue account of $270.98.

Since we have mailed several statements and letters to you, Mr. Lawrence, without any word in return, I'm growing somewhat concerned. Perhaps you are experiencing problems that make it difficult for you to pay this amount all at once. If you are having difficulty making the full payment, please tell me about it--in confidence, of course. I'm sure that we can set up an easy payment plan for you.

We hope to hear from you right away, Mr. Lawrence. I'm sure we'll both be much happier when this matter is resolved to our mutual satisfaction.

Sincerely,

Letter 3 opens a discussion channel. It indicates to the customer that everyone has problems and if he will just explain what his are, perhaps an easier payment plan can be worked out. This letter gives the customer a good chance to discuss things before the seller starts getting tough. Letter 3 might be sent thirty days after the previous one. Some companies at this point begin speeding up the correspondence with shorter intervals between letters.

Collection Letter 4

11.16. An Urgent Message

Dear Mr. Lawrence:

Although we have sent you numerous statements and letters regarding your past-due account of $270.98, we have heard nothing from you.

I'm sure you will understand that we are unable to continue waiting patiently in silence. Therefore, it is essential that this account be settled at once, and we urge you to make the necessary arrangements without delay. If there are circumstances beyond your control, we urge you to tell us about them immediately.

Please put your check in the mail or contact us right away. We must hear from you at once to avoid further action.

Sincerely,

The tone of letter 4 becomes strong and urgent. The essence of the message is that time is running out and that the customer must act quickly or other measures will have to be taken.

Collection Letter 5

11.17. The Special Appeal

Dear Mr. Lawrence:

For several months we have been writing to you about your long past-due account of $270.98. We must know your intentions immediately.

We realize that many overdue accounts are the result of unexpected financial difficulties. In these cases we make every effort to help our customers find a better arrangement for making payment. However, we have not heard from you and cannot offer such help until we know your situation.

Please send us something today. Our company is no longer in a position to continue to maintain your account under the present conditions. If we do not hear from you at once, we will have no choice but to pursue other collection procedures.

Sincerely,

Letter 5 makes an appeal to fear. It says in effect that the time has arrived when the seller can no longer carry the account and must take other collection measures, which usually suggests a collection agency or legal action.

Collection Letter 6

11.18. Prelude to Legal Action

Dear Mr. Lawrence:

Since you did not reply to my letter of January 1, I regret that we must take other action to collect the balance of your past-due account, $270.98.

If we do not receive your check by February 1, you will next hear from the Harris-Blackwell Collection Agency. We hope that you will take this final opportunity to avoid further damage to your credit standing, not to mention the additional costs you may incur if legal action is necessary.

Just send us your check by February 1, and the matter will be resolved before we take this action.

Sincerely,

Letter 6 is the final collection attempt before the account is turned over to a collection agency or lawyer. Usually, the customer is given ten days to two weeks to make payment. To leave no doubt in the customer's mind that the seller means business, the lawyer or collection agency is usually named in this final letter of the series.

12

Sales Promotion

IN one respect, most letters are sales letters in that they sell something—a service, an idea, goodwill, and so on. But the letter specifically intended to promote sales is in a class by itself. Its success, directly or indirectly, can pave the way for company profits; its failure can cause a loss. Sales promotion letters, thus, are often judged by the monetary return they produce; in all cases, they are judged by their effectiveness in stimulating a response. Ideally, these letters are addressed and sent to specific individuals. In large mail campaigns, however, letters may use "Dear Customer," "Dear Friend," or a similar salutation. Computerized mail programs enable mailers to merge individual names and addresses with a standard form letter. The length of the letter may depend on how much printing and postage you can afford. Many writers try to stay within one page to keep costs down and also because they believe their prospects will not read more than a brief message. Other mailers believe that longer letters are more effective.

Sales promotion letters are frequently prepared by specialists, although, even then, the essential information must be given to the preparer. Therefore, you should be familiar with the content and construction of these letters regardless of who prepares them. It may be part of your duties to assist in writing these letters; some may even go out over your own signature (such as 12.4). Or you and your boss may share in the preparation of the sales correspondence, and many of these letters (such as 12.6) will go out over your boss's signature. Since most sales promotion letters are designed first to get attention, second to arouse interest and desire, and third to encourage action, they must follow a particular pattern. This means that the models in this chapter can be used as guides in composing your own letters, and it will be helpful to keep them in your computer file for future use. (Refer to the Model Selector Guide for other letters throughout the book that include promotional messages, such as 11.6 in chapter 11.)

A principal type of sales promotion letter is the introduction of a service of a product. Sometimes this letter includes a sample or some literature (12.3 and 12.4); frequently, the letter just introduces the service, product, or something related to these things, such as a payment plan or the representative servicing a particular area (12.1, 12.2, 12.5, and 12.6).

Once the contact has been made with a customer, a good sales program must plan a variety of follow-ups. These letters vary greatly with circumstances. Sometimes more information must be provided (12.9 and 12.11). Often special tactics must be employed to entice prospective and former customers to purchase something (12.8, 12.10, 12.13, and 12.14). Also, former customers must be contacted in an effort to bring them back (12.12), and it is always important to follow a salesperson's call to a prospective customer with a letter (12.7).

INTRODUCING PRODUCTS AND SERVICES

Before you can introduce a product or service, you must be thoroughly familiar with it and with the person or company you are contacting. This is imperative because sales promotion letters must be very skillfully composed or they will be ineffective. Even in large mail campaigns where you cannot possibly know a specific individual, an effort must be made to select a generally representative audience. The other preliminary information you must have is the nature of the entire sales program. If a series of letters is planned, for example, each one you write must fit properly into this total scheme.

1. Plan your remarks to arouse interest and stimulate action.
2. Describe the product or service being offered and its value to the customer.
3. Explain any special offers or incentives that are available.
4. Leave the door open for further contact.

Models 12.1 through 12.6 illustrate the major types of sales letters that introduce a product, service, salesperson, or some related aspect such as a payment plan.

Introducing a Service

12.1. To Prospective Customer

Dear Mr. Wolf:

May we introduce our new office design and consulting service? We're happy to let you know that Macomb Office Interiors has expanded its line of modern office furniture and accessories and, along with it, has added this new service for customers.

With an experienced staff of office decorators and designers, we can now give you expert advice on all of those things that together can make your office a more pleasant, efficient, and productive unit. Best of all, we can provide this important advice to our customers free of charge. That's right--on any purchase of $100 or more, we will be happy to visit your offices at no additional cost and give you our recommendations for a more efficient layout, better color coordination, improved lighting, and so on.

I'm enclosing a bulletin that describes our expansion, including our new design and consulting service as well as the many new office furnishings we have on the floor. If you would like more information, just call me at 923-7700 or, better yet, stop by our store at 11 Maple Avenue and see our many new selections.

Cordially,

There could be variations of model 12.1. For example, the letter might suggest that the writer will soon telephone for an appointment to have a representative call. It might ask the prospect if he or she would like a free catalog. Or it might invite the prospect to a special showing or open house. Circumstances will dictate specific details of the letter, but all introductions of this type must explain the service and why it should be of interest to the prospect.

Introducing a Product: No Sample

12.2. To Prospective Customer

Dear Mr. Talbert:

Would you like to cut your heat and electric bills drastically this winter? Who wouldn't? That's why more and more people are turning every day to a beautiful cast-iron stove for heating and cooking.

We just acquired a large supply of these magnificent heaters and are introducing them to residents of Morrison County during the month of August with a prewinter sale. Each cast-iron stove--and we have three models to fit any room size--will be available during

August at <u>40 percent off regular retail prices</u> ranging from $429.95 to $1,269.98. This amazing value includes delivery and installation.

These magnificent stoves include a grate basket that holds coal, wood, or charcoal. Doors can be closed when not in use. The cast-iron construction provides more heat than a regular fireplace because of radiation from all sides. Not only are these heaters practical, but they are an attractive addition to any home and fit perfectly in both modern and traditional decors.

Come in today and see for yourself what a truly remarkable value you will find in these beautiful stoves. You'll be glad you did, especially when winter arrives with its inevitable high-cost heating and electric bills. In the meantime, if you have any questions, just call 632-8000 and speak with one of our sales personnel at Otega's Home Furnishings Center.

Sincerely,

When a sample product cannot be sent, and when sales literature is not available, the sales letter must provide enough details to satisfy and interest the prospective customer. Appeal is important in introduction letters. Model 12.2 appeals to the prospect's pocketbook by reminding him of expensive heating and electric bills with conventional heating and cooking methods. The letter closes by explaining how the prospect can learn more about the stoves. Notice the underlining in the body of the letter. Sales writers sometimes call attention to special inducements by underscoring them or using all capitals.

Introducing a Product: Sample Enclosed

12.3. To Prospective Customer

Dear Mrs. Anderson:

Please accept this free sample of the finest 35mm slide-protector pages available today. For many years this distortion-free, clear, vinyl page has been a favorite means of protecting valuable slides and prints for professional photographers; now we are pleased that we can offer this same quality protector page to <u>all</u> camera enthusiasts. What's more, until April 30 we are offering a special introductory discount of <u>10 percent off on any purchase of fifty pages or more</u>.

Your sample of Modern Plastic Corporation's top-loading slide page is designed to hold twenty slides and will fit any standard three-ring binder or album. As the enclosed literature explains, we manufacture pages for all standard-size slides, transparencies, and prints. Although similar pages found in camera stores retail for as much as

$2.50 each, our high-quality, durable plastic pages are available by mail for <u>as little as 70 cents each</u> on orders of fifty pages or more. Think of the savings when you also consider the 10 percent discount being offered until April 30.

Our pages are sent on a satisfaction-guaranteed basis. If you are not completely happy with your purchase, simply return it within thirty days for a full refund. Use the enclosed postage-paid envelope and send us your order today! We'll promptly mail your vinyl protector pages to you postpaid.

Cordially,

P.S. Return your order for fifty pages or more <u>within ten days</u> and you will receive--in addition to the 10 percent discount--<u>one dozen free vinyl protector pages.</u>

If you can afford to send them, sample products, postage-paid envelopes, and descriptive literature are frequently effective in increasing response. Coupons, premiums, and gifts are other types of gimmicks and enclosures employed to stimulate sales. But even when you use enclosures, your letter should sufficiently describe the product and its value to the customer. Model 12.3 also uses a special introductory discount to further encourage sales. The postscript—a common technique in sales letters—is used to make a final tempting offer intended to stimulate a rapid response.

Transmittal Letter to Prospect

12.4. Literature Enclosed

Dear Ms. Daniels:

We're happy to send you the new Pomeroy Catalog of Imports that you requested. This recent issue offers a choice of <u>more than 200 unusual buying opportunities</u> at overseas closeout prices.

Without ever leaving your home you can select quality merchandise from countries all over the world at <u>savings of up to 50 percent</u> off the usual retail prices. All items are insured, and the prices listed in the enclosed catalog represent your total cost--no hidden import fees, no extra insurance fees, just <u>one low price</u> that includes everything.

We hope you'll enjoy the excitement of shopping overseas the easy, inexpensive way. For your convenience, an order form is enclosed in the catalog, and we'll look forward to receiving your first order soon. In the meantime, if you have any other questions, just let me know. We sincerely appreciate your interest in Pomeroy's House of Imports.

Cordially,

Many transmittal letters are little more than brief indications of what is enclosed. Model 12.4 illustrates how a transmittal letter can also be used as a sales promotion letter. Like many other sales letters, this one could be prepared individually or as a form letter that might use a "Dear Customer" salutation.

Introducing a Payment Plan

12.5. To Regular Customer

Dear Mrs. Adams:

Now that the Christmas shopping season is almost here, we want to let you know about a new delayed-payment plan at Davidson's. We hope this new shop-now-and-pay-later plan for our charge customers will make it easier for you to prepare for the holidays without straining your budget during this heavy shopping period.

Here's the way it works: You can stop by our Credit Office the next time you shop at Davidson's and pick up delayed-payment coupons amounting to $300 worth of instant purchases that are not payable until next February. Just present the appropriate number of coupons with each purchase, along with your charge card, and the sales clerk will mark your sales slip for February billing. Your February statement, then, will show all coupon purchases, which will be payable in the usual manner--within thirty days or in monthly installments according to your choice. Of course, during this period you may also use your charge card alone without the coupons for additional purchases.

As always, we look forward to seeing you soon and hope that this year you'll especially enjoy your holiday shopping at Davidson's.

Cordially,

Companies and stores offer a variety of payment plans. Since these plans are designed to increase sales, the letter explaining them should also promote sales. Model 12.5 introduces a special plan for the holidays, and the writer obviously tries to arouse interest in it to encourage the customer to do her holiday shopping at his store.

Paving the Way for a Salesperson's Call

12.6. To Prospective Customer

Dear Mr. Feldman:

We have just added an amazing new set of aluminumware to our cookware line. Since the price of this new set is comparable to the other sets of cookware you carry, your customers should find this a very exciting discovery.

This remarkable new aluminumware has the most durable, nonstick cooking surface I've ever seen. Best of all, unlike other finishes, the interior can't be damaged by metal utensils; yet it cleans just as easily as more sensitive nonstick surfaces. The finish is beautiful-- heavy gauge aluminum exteriors with rich, pewter-look interiors--and each of the eleven pieces in a set has heat-resistant black handles and knobs. I'm enclosing some manufacturing specs that describe each piece in the set and offer other market data. In all, the eleven-piece set retails for about $149.95 ($179.95 separately). However, sets are available to you at our usual 40 to 60 percent factory markdown, depending on quantities ordered.

Bob Willis, one of our sales representatives, will be in your area the week of October 10 and will contact you before then to see when it would be convenient to stop by to show you a complete set. I just know you're going to be as impressed as I am with this magnificent cookware. In the meantime, do call if you have any questions.

Best regards,

Different approaches can be used to pave the way for a salesperson's visit. For instance, if the customer does not know the sales representative, the letter might focus on introducing the person, rather than the product (see model 6.7 in chapter 6.) In model 12.6 the writer prefers to introduce the new product, and thus the letter is a typical introduction to a product, except that it closes by identifying the representative who will be calling on the customer.

WRITING FOLLOW-UP SALES LETTERS

Seldom do first letters or calls by sales representatives produce enough sales to justify no further effort. Thus the follow-up letter is essential in a sales program. Some companies plan a series of letters, assuming it may take as many as four to six contacts before adequate sales result. The follow-up letter should contain the same vital information covered in the initial letter of introduction.

1. Describe again the product or service being offered and again stress its value to the customer.

2. Repeat any special offers or incentives that are available.

3. Provide any additional or new information that may arouse the customer's interest and stimulate action.

4. Leave the door open for still further contact.

Models 12.7 through 12.14 illustrate the variety of sales promotion situations requiring a follow-up letter.

Following a Salesperson's Call

12.7. To Prospective Customer

Dear Mr. Samuels:

Our representative Joe Devonshire sends his thanks along with mine for the time you spent with him last Tuesday. The information you gave him about your operations has been a tremendous help to us in determining how we might be of assistance to your company.

It's true that your semiautomated bookkeeping and associated re-cord-keeping system is unnecessarily complicated and cumbersome. Naturally, this creates added costs for you in staff time and year-end auditing expenses. If we were to devise a more appropriate computerized system for your particular operation, the savings to you each year could amount to as much as $11,300 in in-house staff time as well as a reduction in auditing costs of at least $3,000. That's a potential of $14,300 in total annual savings. I'm enclosing a detailed report that explains this possibility more fully.

The most efficient procedure would be for us to write a completely new program for you at the time we do your annual audit. The cost of devising and implementing the software at that time would be $1,950. With the new system, your savings in year one alone would cover this cost and perhaps leave thousands to spare.

I'll telephone you in a couple weeks, Mr. Samuels, to see if I can add anything to the enclosed proposal. In the meantime, you can reach me at 493-0120 if you have any questions.

Best regards,

Model 12.7 is a follow-up of a representative's call that gets right to the point: It suggests what service the customer needs and the cost of that service. Specific information is presented in an enclosed proposal. Even this to-the-point type of follow-up, however, leaves the door open for another contact in case the customer still does not agree to the proposal.

After Rejection of Merchandise

12.8. Article Returned

Dear Ms. Parsons:

I'm sorry to learn that you want to return the TLT auto electronic typewriter you were using on a trial basis. Our sales representative mentioned that you thought the advanced features were insufficient for your needs.

It occurs to me that you might be much happier with our new TLT-10 model. This machine has all the features of the TLT--and more. It is larger, is heavier, and is designed for rapid, ultraprecision, high-quality type production.

I'm enclosing some literature on the new TLT-10, and I've asked Bob Wilson, our sales representative, to telephone you next week. I know that he will be happy to discuss the advantages of the TLT-10 for your situation and will be glad to leave a machine with you to try for a week.

We sincerely appreciate your interest in our typewriters, Ms. Parsons. Now that we have a better idea of your expectations, I know that we can show you exactly the right machine for your needs.

Cordially,

Model 12.8 illustrates a follow-up (after a rejection of merchandise) that does not give up. When a customer rejects a product, companies and their sales representatives must quickly look for alternative products or some adjustment that will satisfy the customer. Thus these follow-ups must present an appealing option immediately, before the customer goes elsewhere and purchases a competitor's product.

After Request for More Information

12.9. Interested Customer

Dear Ms. Eisenstadt:

I was very happy to learn that several persons in your department are considering attending our Advanced Photography Workshop in Buffalo on May 19. The 3:45 p.m. session on advanced darkroom techniques will, indeed, cover the area in which your staff is most interested: creative techniques. These are but a few of the topics that will be discussed:

--Previsualization

--Designing a multiple print

--Exposure and development for each element

--Procedures for printing in new elements

--Posterization, Kodalith masking, and bas relief

--How to add new dimensions to your pictures

The workshop will provide an excellent opportunity for professionals to meet with other professionals. Generally, it will be a day of ultra-intensive training in the most advanced commercial techniques--something too good to miss!

I'm enclosing a dozen copies of our final program, with registration and hotel accommodation forms, for you to distribute among your staff. Since registration is limited to the first 100 enrollments, I would urge you to submit the forms as soon as possible.

Let me know if I can offer any further information, Ms. Eisenstadt. Otherwise, I'll look forward to meeting you and your staff on May 18 in Buffalo.

Cordially,

When a prospect requests information, he or she is obviously interested in the product or service being offered. The response, then, should be prompt, courteous, informative, and appealing.

Invitation to Use Other Products

12.10. Following a Purchase

Dear Mr. Carlton:

Thank you very much for your order for twenty steel shelving units. We sincerely appreciate this opportunity to be of service to you.

The units you selected are our most popular space organizers. I know you'll be pleased with this exceptionally practical and durable shelving. High quality and low cost are features typical of our full line of space-saving storage units. A copy of our latest catalog is enclosed to show you some other products that could help you achieve maximum efficiency in storage the economical way. Notice in particular our pull-drawer storage files, literature trays, high-stack files, and flip-top storage files. These items are all designed to complement the steel shelving units you have chosen.

Please let me know if there is any way I can help you plan a more efficient, convenient, and economical filing and storage system for your business. It would be a pleasure to work with you, Mr.

Carlton, and I'm delighted to welcome you as a customer of Modern Business Products, Inc.

Cordially,

Most companies take advantage of one sale to encourage more sales. A customer who has purchased one product is a good candidate for more purchases. Model 12.10 (1) thanks the customer, (2) introduces similar products that might interest the customer, (3) offers to be of help in planning and selecting other products, and (4) welcomes the new customer.

Offering Additional Information

12.11. To a Customer

Dear Mrs. Hartley:

Early this month we let you know that LaRue's House of Art had acquired an original collection of hand-crafted colonial figures. Since then we have had numerous inquiries about the figures, especially in regard to the colors represented in the collection. As a discerning collector, I'm certain this aspect is of particular interest to you.

The thirteen sculptures are all hand-painted in full color, just like the native-lands collection you saw on display last month in our showroom. I'm enclosing a color print of the new colonial collection to show you how vivid and realistic the colors are on these superbly crafted figures. As you can see, the combination of nine colors, hand-painted with the finest detail, gives exceptional authenticity to each lifelike colonial sculpture. The collection is truly a remarkable and beautiful treasure.

Since we have only this one original colonial collection, do let me know right away if you would like to have me hold it for you, Mrs. Hartley. In the meantime, if I can offer any additional information, you can reach me at 852-7300, Monday through Saturday.

Cordially,

Follow-ups are often designed to provide additional information with each succeeding contact. Model 12.11, which takes this approach, provides new facts about the product being offered, even though the customer did not ask for the information. Naturally, the additional information must in some way make the product more desirable and thus arouse the customer's interest.

Contacting Former Customer

12.12. To Renew Service

Dear Mr. Atkins:

We haven't heard from you for nearly six months and have missed working with you on your mail campaigns. It was always a pleasure to handle your addressing and mailing needs, and we very much appreciated your business.

I hope nothing serious has happened to discourage you from continuing to use our service. If something has escaped my attention, please do let me know. It has always been our policy to offer the best service possible, and I'm always prepared to take whatever steps are necessary to insure that our customers are fully satisfied. If there's anything we can do to satisfy your needs or help you in any way, Mr. Atkins, I would welcome an opportunity to talk to you about it.

Please do write or call me at 632-4000 sometime soon. I'd enjoy hearing from you again.

Cordially,

Letters soliciting business from former customers must be written with care. If you are unaware of any previous problem, it obviously would be a mistake to give the impression you gave poor service in the past. That could suggest that poor service is so typical of your company that you automatically assume it is the cause of a customer's withdrawal. If you can think of nothing for which you should apologize, avoid an apologetic tone. Stress your desire to satisfy the customer and try to find out why the customer left, but keep the tone of your letter positive.

Requesting Referral

12.13. Regular Customer

Dear Mr. Jenkins:

In this fast-paced world of overcrowded cities and roads we all yearn for a taste of the good life--getting away from it all and enjoying the wonders of nature. Some of us--like you--have found a way to enjoy nature year-round without even leaving home. I'm referring to your recent purchase of our vinyl-paneled greenhouse. Since you're one of our regular customers, I know how much you appreciate and enjoy the wonder of beautiful growing and thriving plants, right in your own backyard.

Mason's Greenery has been a leader in the field of indoor-outdoor plant and gardening supplies for more than a decade. We believe our greenhouses are the best available at prices that make them realistic for almost any size income. Moreover, as you know, all our gardening products are backed by guarantees. We also stock a full line of accessories--pots, benches, shelves, plants--for all our greenhouses.

We would like to tell others about the pleasure of year-round gardening in a Mason's greenhouse. If you have friends or relatives who share your enthusiasm for this wonderful hobby, we would like to let them know about our products and service. If you have no objection, just write the names and addresses that come to mind on the enclosed postage-paid card and mail it today. There's a space to indicate whether or not you want to have your name mentioned.

Many thanks for your help and cooperation, Mr. Jenkins. We'll be looking forward to seeing you soon again at Mason's Greenery.

Cordially,

Companies often ask for referrals from customers since this is an excellent means of locating prospects. The letter may or may not offer something in return. Model 12.13 makes no offer, unlike model 12.14, which includes a special incentive if the customer will actually contact friends and relatives.

Asking Customer to Join Sales Force

12.14. With Special Incentive

Dear Mrs. Lane:

How would you like to earn valuable gifts from McDaniels' Stemware Shop? Since you have been one of our regular customers for more than five years, I know how much you appreciate our lovely glassware. You are certainly well qualified to comment on the quality and beautify of McDaniels' stemware and glass serving sets.

Knowing your familiarity with our products, we were wondering if you would like to become a neighborhood representative of McDaniels--showing friends, neighbors, and relatives the pieces you already have and others we would provide to you for showings. Sales resulting from these contacts would entitle you to free selections from our stemware and glassware serving sets.

In the hope that you will like the idea of earning free gifts in such an easy and enjoyable way--right from your own home--I'm enclosing a booklet describing the procedure of becoming a McDaniels neighborhood representative. After reading the booklet, all you need to do is sign and mail the enclosed postage-paid card. Your first shipment of items to show will soon be delivered, and you can begin earning your free selections of stemware and serving sets right away.

It has been a pleasure to have you as one of our regular customers during the past years, Mrs. Lane, and I hope that now we can also count you among our regular neighborhood representatives.

Cordially,

Model 12.14 illustrates a common sales technique: asking customers to show merchandise to friends and relatives in exchange for free gifts. Sometimes the free gifts are offered just in exchange for the names and addresses of friends and relatives.

Part

II

MEMOS

13

Memos That Give Information

MEMOS were once regarded as strictly a form of *internal* business communication. In that respect they have been less a public relations tool than the external letter and more a management and administrative tool. But today the memo format is also prominent in external correspondence.

Memos, speed messages, note paper, preprinted forms, and other informal types of communication are familiar sights in the modern business office. To help cope with a massive flood of information, companies are seeking such timesaving formats at every turn. Not only does the memo usually take less time to prepare than a formal letter, it also can be prepared on less expensive (sometimes smaller or different-sized) paper than formal letterhead stationery. However, many memos are prepared by computer and printed out on the same paper as that used for a business letter.

In deciding whether to use a memo or letter format, the choice in part is one of intent: What impression do you want to make? Can the correspondence be informal or must it appear more formal, for example, with an inside address? Beyond that, the memo is the preferred in-house vehicle for conveying objective, factual information. Many offices also use this simpler format for certain outside contacts: (1) for routine transactions, such as processing orders, transmitting material, confirming arrangements and receipts, and making inquiries; and (2) for easy, rapid communication with business friends, longtime customers, and other persons with whom you have developed a casual, friendly working relationship and with whom you must exchange objective, factual information.

You will write and send many of the memos illustrated in this chapter (such as 13.16). You may draft others (such as 13.12) for your boss. Even when your boss drafts the memo (such as 13.24), you may be expected to refine and polish it. Keep all of the memos in your computer file for use on future occasions.

This chapter concentrates on memos that primarily *give* information. Chapter 14 deals with those that primarily make a request.

1. Present your facts clearly and objectively, in a logical sequence.

2. Be concise but offer all essential information.

3. Indicate if any response is expected from the recipient.

Ten categories of memos that give information are discussed here, including analytical memos (13.1-13.3), announcements and replies (13.4-13.13), follow-ups and reminders (13.14-13.16), explanations (13.17-13.24), recommendations (13.25-13.27), orders (13.28-13.30), instructions (13.31-13.33), reports (13.34-13.38), confirmations (13.39-13.43), and transmittal memos (13.44-13.47). Notice that although the basic purpose of these memos is to *give* information, many of them also include a *request* for something.

WRITING ANALYTICAL MEMOS

The analytical memo evaluates something—a person, product, service, or situation. It reports on the subject objectively, clearly, and concisely. The memo itself may contain all essential facts, or certain data (if lengthy or if in the form of tables, charts, or the like) may be provided in an attachment. (Notice the use of subheads in some instances to increase organizational clarity.) Models 13.1 through 13.3 are examples of typical in-house analytical memos.

Employee

13.1. Performance

TO: Melvin Anderson

ANITA REESE--PERFORMANCE ANALYSIS

Here's the performance evaluation of Anita Reese you requested. Also attached are detailed rating charts concerning her (1) educational background, (2) job skills, and (3) personal characteristics.

EDUCATIONAL BACKGROUND: Ms. Reese is a high school graduate and a graduate of Wilton Secretarial School. She also has completed miscellaneous night courses in bookkeeping, data processing, and business communication.

JOB SKILLS: Ms. Reese has excellent abilities in word processing, filing, use of office machines, and simple bookkeeping. She has moderate to poor abilities in telephone communication and receptionist duties.

PERSONAL CHARACTERISTICS: Ms. Reese is neat and businesslike in appearance. She is a quiet, industrious, and careful worker, with above-average concern for detail and accuracy. She prefers to work alone and avoid contact with others and is generally ineffective in situations requiring telephone or other personal exchange.

SUMMARY: Ms. Reese is highly proficient in all office skills and duties with the exception of telephone and other personal communication. Therefore, I recommend that she be retained and advanced at appropriate intervals in positions where minimal personal contact is required.

Let me know if you need further information, Mel.

Machine

13.2. Performance

TO: Joe Carter

FAX MACHINE

The Martell fax in Mr. Brownley's office is still functioning erratically. We have had service representatives look at it and adjust it on several occasions without success. As yet no one has discovered how to control the imaging function, with the result that copies have been either too faint or too dark.

I suggest that we have the Martell representative pick up the machine immediately and replace it with one that is operating properly. If you agree, please ask the representative to provide another machine for our temporary use if there will be a delay in receiving a permanent replacement.

Thanks very much, Joe.

Tests and Interview

13.3. Results

TO: Kevin Bradley

GERALD McKINNEY: APPLICATION FOR EMPLOYMENT

Attached are test scores and the results of my interview with Gerald McKinney, who is applying for the position of data-processing training instructor in our department.

BACKGROUND: Age 27, married with two children, B.A. in economics, four years' experience teaching data processing at Seaton Technical Institute.

INTERVIEW: Mr. McKinney was well prepared and organized and supported his written application with a strong, personal desire to join our organization and progress within it. He demonstrated a good understanding of a company instructor's duties and a thorough knowledge of data processing. His oral presentation was pleasing and effective.

TESTS: Mr. McKinney scored very high on each of our departmental knowledge and skills tests in data processing and instruction.

RECOMMENDATION: Mr. McKinney is a highly qualified candidate for the training-instructor position and should be given serious consideration along with other exceptionally well qualified applicants. He would be an asset to our organization and every effort should be made to place him in this or another suitable position.

If I can add anything, Kevin, just let me know.

PREPARING ANNOUNCEMENTS AND REPLIES

Announcements are prepared in a variety of formats: letters, memos, news releases, bulletins, cards, and brochures. Content and audience will dictate which format to use. For example, an announcement of an open house might be prepared in the format of a formal invitation (see models 15.1 and 15.13 in chapter 15); a timely announcement, such as the development of a revolutionary new product, might be sent as a press release (see models 16.1 and 16.14 in chapter 16); an announcement that contains other information directed to an individual would best be sent as a letter or memo.

Meeting Notice

13.4. Sales Meeting

TO: All Sales Representatives

JULY MEETING

The next sales meeting will be held on Monday, July 12, from 10 a.m. until 3 p.m. at the Country Motor Lodge, Route 5, in Kingston. Lunch will be provided.

An agenda will be mailed to you on June 30. If you have any items to be included, please send them to my secretary by June 29.

I would appreciate hearing from you right away if you're unable to attend. Thanks very much.

New Policy Procedure

13.5. Of Company

TO: Department Managers

CAFETERIA SHIFTS

Since our work force has been expanding, so have the lines in the cafeteria. To solve this annoying problem, we have decided to serve lunch in three specific shifts: 11:30 a.m., 12:00 noon, and 12:30 p.m.

Please arrange within your own department which employees will be assigned to each luncheon shift, giving them a choice if possible. To avoid an overload in one of the shifts, however, please try to assign about the same number of people to each period.

I sincerely appreciate your cooperation in implementing this new procedure. Let's hope that we've seen the last of those long and tedious cafeteria lines.

Company Event

13.6. Party

TO: All Employees

SUMMER PICNIC, AUGUST 4

The directors of J. T. Anderson and Company are pleased to announce that our annual summer picnic will be held on Friday, August 4, from 11 a.m. until 4 p.m. at Maxwell Park.

A picnic lunch will be provided for each employee and his or her guest. After lunch there will be a choice of good conversation or outdoor recreational activities--tennis, softball, swimming, and much more--for everyone, concluding at 4 p.m. with a special drawing for a new color TV!

So that we can make appropriate luncheon arrangements, please let Jeanne Hollis in the Public Relations Department know whether you plan to attend and if you will bring a guest.

We're looking forward to seeing everyone on August 4.

Promotion

13.7. Of Employee

TO: Members of the Art Department

ASSISTANT ART DIRECTOR APPOINTMENT

It's a pleasure to announce the appointment of Robert Carstairs, Jr., as assistant art director at the Lewis Press. He will fill the position left open by Jerry Kincaid, who recently moved to the East Coast.

Bob, who just completed his seventh year at Lewis Press, is very familiar with all aspects of production in our department, having handled each function--pasteup, stripping, camera, and so on--at some time. His solid background and full understanding of our varied needs and problems make him exceptionally well qualified to handle the challenges that confront the assistant director every day.

I know he will welcome your full cooperation and consideration as he assumes his new duties. We all wish him much success.

Dismissal

13.8. Of Employee

TO: Members of the Service Department

CUSTOMER REPRESENTATIVE POSITIONS

This is to let you know that the employment of David Thurston as customer representative at Wright Motors was terminated effective October 1. We hope to announce his replacement by the end of this month.

Our service manager, Bill Grady, may be calling on some of you to serve temporarily as customer representative until we have a replacement. We hope you will give Bill your complete cooperation during this time so that our customers will continue to receive full and thoughtful attention without interruption.

Thanks for your help and understanding.

Prices and Rates

13.9. Increase

TO: Carla Brownell

RATE CHANGE

As we discussed by telephone this morning, please take the necessary steps to institute the following new advertising rates for the Daily Marketer:

Ad Size	New Rate (B&W)
One page	$1,600
Two-thirds page	1,475
One-half page horiz.	1,400
One-half page vert.	1,420
One-third page horiz.	1,320
One-third page vert.	1,320
One-sixth page	1,150
(Color addit.)	(No charge)

As soon as you've had an opportunity to draft a letter of notification to our advertisers and prospects, I'd like to see a copy of it. Also, could you let me know when the new rate cards will be ready?

Thanks very much, Carla.

Task Assignment

13.10. To Employee

TO: Edna Stahling

TOUR ARRANGEMENTS

I just received a tour request from Walt Nyland, general manager of the Patterson Company in Grand Rapids, Michigan. He would like to have four of his sales staff tour our pattern-making and sewing departments on March 11.

I'd like to have you handle the arrangements for the visiting group. This will involve the following steps:

1. Contact our department heads to establish a time for the tour and to arrange for a guide in each department.
2. Select someone to greet the visitors, usher them from one department to another, and see them off at the conclusion.
3. Contact Mr. Nyland to discuss the proposed tour plan and to determine if he would like assistance in travel or hotel arrangements. (See the enclosed letter from him for his address and telephone number.)
4. Confirm final details with all concerned parties.

Let me know if you have any questions, Edna, and good luck!

Commendation

13.11. Of Employee Performance

TO: Benjamin Miltown

W. D. ALLISON ACCOUNT

The third-quarter figures are in, and it's official--we passed a million dollar sales volume on the Allison account!

Your staff has done a magnificent job in handling this account, Ben, and I know this is a result of your expert guidance. It has taken a lot of time and effort to reach this goal, but you may be certain that the contribution of you and your staff has been duly noted.

Congratulations to all of you from all of us at headquarters!

Thank You

13.12. For Project Approval

TO: Dennis Hazlitt

METRIC SYSTEM

I was delighted to receive your authorization to convert our shipping department to the metric system by the end of this fiscal year. I am certain that this change will greatly simplify dealings with our foreign customers.

Many thanks for the green light, Dennis. I'll begin right away and will keep you posted on our progress.

Acknowledgment

13.13. *Of Procedural Change*

TO: Michelle Macomb

EXECUTIVE BULLETIN

Thank you for your May 7 directive concerning the bulletin schedule. We are making the necessary adjustments today to convert to a bimonthly schedule, and the next issue will be distributed on June 1.

SENDING FOLLOW-UPS AND REMINDERS

Many follow-ups and reminders are no more than brief, factual messages. Often, in such cases it would be a waste of secretarial time and expensive stationery to prepare a formal letter. The memo is ideal for these situations, as you can see in models 13.14 through 13.16. (See chapter 4 for models of reminder and follow-up letters.) In certain instances this format can be used for external as well as internal follow-ups (such as model 13.16).

Deadline Approaching

13.14. *For Report*

TO: Maxine Arnold

CUSTOMER SURVEY

Just a reminder that the customer survey report you're preparing is due March 11. I'd appreciate it if you would let me know the present status of the project. Thanks, Max.

Awaiting Information

13.15. *Agenda*

TO: Donald Fox

AGENDA, EXECUTIVE COMMITTEE MEETING

The Executive Committee meeting agenda is complete except for your item regarding the research proposal. Any luck yet in getting the information we need? Since the deadline for mailing the agenda is November 5, I'll need the proposal details from you by noon on the 4th--at the latest.

Thanks, Don.

Shipment Overdue

13.16. Office Supplies

TO: Kraus Business Forms, Inc.

ORDER FOR SUPPLIES (P.O. 060112)

On April 9 we ordered from you 5,000 #MACS Management Action Control Sheets (see enclosed copy of our purchase order) to be delivered by May 15.

We are in urgent need of the control sheets, but the shipment has not yet arrived. Would you please let me know right away whether the shipment has gone out and when you expect that it will arrive? If the order has not yet been sent, please handle it on a rush basis and let me know the expected delivery date.

Thank you.

MAKING EXPLANATIONS

Explanations are part of the daily fare in any business office. The letter format is more appropriate in many instances, particularly in external contacts that also involve an apology or that in some way involve sensitive customer relations. But the memo is suitable when the explanation is basically routine or factual, as it is in models 13.17 through 13.23. Model 13.23 illustrates the use of the memo format in external communications for a routine notice addressed only to "Purchasing Agent."

For Action

13.17. Of Company

TO: All Supervisors

TV MONITORING SYSTEM

We will soon be installing a visual monitoring system in all cautionary work areas at the mill. A pamphlet is enclosed that explains the operation of this new system.

The system provides twenty-four-hours-a-day visual contact with all work areas where full safety measures are needed. The contact is channeled to each supervisor's workstation and to the office of the floor manager. This visual monitoring device will alert us to dangers and potential accidents--before they occur--that we might otherwise miss. So that there will be no misunderstanding, I suggest you inform your crew right away that the TV monitoring system is a <u>safety measure</u> intended strictly to provide greater <u>protection for employees</u> in cautionary work areas and that it will be used for no other purpose.

If you have any questions, just let me know. I appreciate your help in letting our employees know about this new safety device.

Apology for Error

13.18. In Cost Estimate

TO: Donald Summers

SHIPPING COST ESTIMATE

Don, you are absolutely correct--the cost estimate I sent inadvertently omitted a zero in the figure of $124. Clearly, it should have been $1,240. I'm thankful that your careful review caught this error before it was incorporated into the department's budget.

Please accept my apologies for the mistake. I'll make certain that it doesn't happen again.

Reason for New Policy-Procedure

13.19. In Office

TO: Administrative and Secretarial Staff

TIME-WORK STUDIES

In the past month we have discovered some instances in which a duplication of effort has occurred in this office and other instances in which certain duties seemed unnecessarily time consuming and cumbersome. Apparently, it is time to review our respective functions to see how our tasks and procedures can be improved.

Attached is a one-week supply of daily time-work analysis forms. For one week, I would like to have each of you record on these forms the work you do and the time you spend doing it. Please include everything, from sharpening pencils to typing a report. At the end of the week, if you will return the completed forms to me, I will prepare individual activity summaries. Once we have this type of information, we can easily spot the areas where we need to streamline our procedures and eliminate overlap and duplication of effort. To insure that we don't slip back into our old habits and old problems,

I would like to repeat this type of analysis periodically, perhaps once every six months or once a year.

I sincerely appreciate your cooperation and am certain that with your help we can soon have our office running smoothly and efficiently.

Cause of a Problem

13.20. In Scheduling

TO: Dan Polaski

GIFT HOUSE CATALOG SCHEDULE

The dummy for the Gift House catalog just arrived, and your job ticket (no. 6177) states that the customer wants to see a proof in two weeks. This presents a problem. We just started a large town report for Pine Hills--also due in two weeks.

Ordinarily, we could handle both with some overtime, but Roy Parker is on vacation this week and Joyce Kummel is still in the hospital. Since we're short-handed, there's no way we can finish the catalog in two weeks. Unless you can quickly find us some temporary help, we'll have to let the Gift House know that it will be at least three weeks before its proof is ready.

Please let me know what you think, Dan. Thanks very much.

Reason for Resignation

13.21. Of Committee Chair

TO: Anne Pascal

CONFERENCE COMMITTEE CHAIR

This will confirm my resignation as Conference Committee chair, as I indicated to you by telephone yesterday. As much as I enjoyed the committee activities, my new duties as marketing manager will take me into the field for long periods, and I won't be available often enough to do justice to the position.

I'll be happy to help the new chair in any way that I can. In the meantime, here is my committee file for you to present to the new appointee. Let me know if you need anything else from me, Anne.

Best wishes for a successful conference next spring.

Need for Cooperation

13.22. Of Employees

TO: All Employees

PARKING LOT CONSTRUCTION

I'm certain that you've all noticed the poor condition of our parking lot. As a result of an unusually severe winter, the surface is a mass of cracks and holes. Since this is a heavy vacation month and fewer cars are in the lot, it seems like the ideal time to resurface the entire lot.

We have arranged for repair and resurfacing work to begin on Wednesday, July 6, and conclude on Saturday, July 9. Unfortunately, from Wednesday through Friday it will be necessary to keep all cars out of the lot. Therefore, we will have to park our cars along the street during those three days. Some of you may even want to form car pools to cut down the number of vehicles needing parking spaces along the street.

As much as we all regret the temporary inconvenience, it will be a pleasure to have a much-improved parking lot after the resurfacing is completed. Your cooperation in making this possible will be greatly appreciated.

Shipment Delayed

13.23. To Customer

TO: Purchasing Agent

YOUR ORDER NO. 913: PORTABLE WELDERS

We are sorry to let you know that the six portable welders you ordered on August 11 are temporarily out of stock. However, they have been back-ordered and will be shipped promptly on September 1.

We regret any inconvenience this delay may cause. If there is any way that we can be of help in the meantime, please let us know.

Need to Cut Costs

13.24. In Supplies

TO: Adele Shipley

COST OF SUPPLIES

After reviewing our latest income statement, showing a marked decline in third-quarter profits, I have targeted certain areas for immediate steps in cost control. One of those areas in which we must reduce our costs is in the purchase of equipment parts and supplies.

Therefore, I am asking that you meet with Rob Baldwin this week and prepare a new budget implementing strategies to accommodate a $30,000 or greater reduction for the first quarter of the next fiscal year. I'll need your revised figures by November 1.

I know this is a tall order, Adele, but I'm sure you will find a way to institute the necessary controls. I wish our financial position were brighter, but under the circumstances we must take strong measures to keep the company on sound economic footing and thereby protect the accounts and jobs that depend on us every day.

I'll look forward to hearing from you soon. Best wishes.

MAKING RECOMMENDATIONS

Certain recommendations are essentially in-house minireports or miniproposals. These recommendations, when they are primarily factual and objective, are particularly well suited for the memo format. Models 13.25 through 13.27 are examples of such messages. See also 13.38 and the model pages from a formal report in chapter 16.

Proposal

13.25. For New Department

TO: John Norris

PROPOSED PUBLIC RELATIONS DEPARTMENT

Here are the preliminary recommendations I promised concerning the proposed Public Relations Department.

OBJECTIVE: To handle our public relations activities more effectively by collecting them in one office and having the same person be responsible for them at all times. At present, PR duties are scattered from office to office. There is too much overlap and inefficiency in collecting and generating information. Moreover, the PR function suffers since now it is always an extracurricular activity for everyone and thus is frequently neglected. The time each of us would save by moving these functions out of our own offices would more than pay for the services of one productive PR person.

ACTIVITIES: The major functions that should be transferred to this new office are as follows:

1. Media contact (press releases, ads, press conferences)
2. Newsletter production (quarterly company bulletin)
3. Customer relations (complaints, special programs)
4. Survey supervision (assisting marketing and sales)
5. Research (miscellaneous fact finding)
6. Audiovisual supervision (assisting other departments)

There might be other activities that we would want to add to this list later, but the above six points could be considered the basis for a job definition.

PERSONNEL: The reports I've received indicate that one person could handle the PR work, using our word processing pool for support. This person could be selected from within our company (preferable in terms of knowing our operations) or brought in from the outside (might find someone with a better PR background). We should discuss this aspect with the personnel director.

CONCLUSION: We could greatly improve our public relations if we established a separate Public Relations Department. Functions now handled in a fragmented way in various offices would be centralized in the new PR office, thereby insuring greater efficiency and effectiveness.

Let me know if you would like to pursue this idea, John. I'll be glad to provide further details and discuss it at your convenience.

Recommendation for Change

13.26. In Methods

TO: Lois Van Dyke

SUPPLIES INVENTORY CONTROL

I would like to suggest another method for maintaining and replenishing supplies in the storage closet. At present, there are three of us on this floor who remove supplies at random, which often results in unexpected depletion of some supplies and the constant need to replenish them on a rush basis.

To introduce some sort of warning system, I recommend that supplies be stacked from front to back on shelves so that the total number of any item on hand can be written boldly on the front package. Each person who removes any of them should cross out that number and write the current remaining number on the front package.

To further help us, we should establish for each item the point at which it is time to reorder and leave a typed list showing this in the storage closet. Each person who removes anything should check the remaining number of the item on hand with the reorder number on the list. For instance, perhaps after someone removes 1,000 letterheads there are 5,000 left and the list shows that we should reorder when the supply is down to 5,000. That person then should immediately notify you that it is time to reorder stationery.

The control I'm suggesting should eliminate at least a large part of our problem of unexpected depletions. If you would like to try this method, I'll be glad to set it up and get us started. Just let me know.

To Solve a Problem

13.27. In Office

TO: Jack Webster

IMPROVING THE RECEPTION AREA

Janice and I have been discussing a persistent problem in the reception area. Although the function of greeting visitors has been assigned to Janice, the reception room doesn't have a wall space near the door where her desk can be placed. Thus both Janice and I have our desks close together toward the back of the room. The result is that visitors sometimes walk directly to my desk, before Janice can get their attention. This means that I have many unnecessary interruptions each day, which sometimes makes it difficult to accomplish anything.

Since the reception room isn't suitable for repositioning our desks, we want to recommend another solution: have a sign made for Janice's desk (or near it) that says "Receptionist" or "Information." It should be large enough for a visitor to spot instantly upon entering the room (e.g., 4" x 15") but not so large or awkward that it takes up important work space.

Please let us know if we may follow through with this idea. Thanks.

PROCESSING ORDERS

Orders are processed in many ways; often, when substantial numbers are involved, they are processed with special forms such as requisitions, purchase orders, and confirmation forms (see 17.14 and 17.15 in chapter 17). When very few orders are processed in an office, and special forms are not used, the letter (see chapter 2) or memo format is typical. Many routine orders can be processed easily and rapidly by using the memo format, as illustrated in models 13.28 and 13.29.

Placing Orders

13.28. For Supplies

TO: Office Accessories, Inc.

ORDER FOR NAME PLATES

Please send us the following name plates, to be billed to Dempsy Products, 113 Church Street, Marlborough, MA 01752:

One (1) #JAR-MT, 2" x 8" clear acrylic name plate, $18.50, for BEN RANDALL

One (1) #XTP-JV, 2" x 8" self-adhesive walnut acrylic door plate, $16.95, for BEN RANDALL

One (1) #ROC-LN, 1" x 3" black acrylic name tag with white lettering in all capitals, $12.50, for BEN RANDALL, BUSINESS MANAGER

These items should be sent to the attention of Susan Wyatt, Room 410, at Dempsy Products. Thank you.

Changing Order

13.29. For Service

TO: Venus Office Machines

MAINTENANCE CONTRACT 0710943-66

We would like to change the maintenance arrangement for our model 8 Venus copier from a one-year to a three-year contract. We understand that there is no reduction in the annual charge with a longer term contract but that we are protected against servicing price increases during this time.

Please send an invoice for the additional two-year period to Mason Travel Service, 911 24th Street, Chicago, IL 60609. Thank you.

Canceling Order

13.30. For Equipment

TO: TLC Computers

ORDER NO. 6301-ZF, JULY 7, 19--

Please cancel our order for one 3 1/2-inch floppy disk drive. After evaluating our requirements, we have concluded that our 5 1/4-inch drive will be sufficient for our present needs. We do, however, expect to upgrade our equipment later this year and will contact you again at that time.

Thank you.

PROVIDING INSTRUCTIONS

Instructions represent another category of communication appropriate for the memo format. Many instructions, particularly if they are in-house communications, are primarily brief, factual messages that do not require a formal letter. Models 13.31 through 13.33 are examples of memos that provide instructions (13.32 and 13.33 are external communications).

Instructing Employees

13.31. About New Procedure

TO: Shipping Clerks

GIFT ENCLOSURES

From November 1 through January 31 the following free gifts are to be enclosed with each customer's purchase:

Orders up to $10--Small memo calendar

Orders $10-$25--Large wall calendar

Orders over $25--Pocket calendar in vinyl wallet

Calendars, which are already wrapped, should be packaged carefully with the customers' orders so that they will not be bent, crushed, or otherwise damaged during shipment. Our shipping supervisor, Joe Nichols, recommends placing the calendars at the bottom of each box with protective cardboard positioned on top of the calendar before other items are enclosed.

If you have any questions or problems with the gift calendars, please contact Joe Nichols in the Shipping Department right away. Thank you.

Operating Instructions

13.32. For Film Copier

TO: Balsam Insurance Agency

MODEL 750 SPECTRUM PROCESSOR OPERATING INSTRUCTIONS

The model 750 Spectrum Processor is particularly easy to operate. If you follow the simple instructions for operation and maintenance provided in the enclosed booklet, you will enjoy many years of trouble-free processing. There are no messy chemicals to worry about. A simple dusting every so often is all that is required. Briefly, these are the steps to follow in making quality copies:

1. Turn the ON-OFF switch to ON and let the machine warm up.
2. Place a sheet of transparent copy paper, glossy side up, on top of the original to be copied.
3. Lay the two pieces on the exposure plate, with the transparent sheet next to the plate. Close the lid.
4. Set the exposure knob at number 6 (you may want to try several settings to find the one you prefer) and press the knob.
5. After the light goes off, place the transparent sheet, glossy side up, on the clear side of the white copy paper.
6. Insert the two sheets into the feeder slot and wait for your copy to come out. Discard the transparent sheet upon removal.
7. Turn the ON-OFF switch to OFF.

That's all there is to it--a fast and easy process that produces copies of amazing clarity. Should you have any questions, however, please do let us know. We appreciate having you as a customer and want to be certain you are receiving the best results possible with your new Spectrum Processor.

For Meeting Location

13.33. Out of Town

TO: Members of the Conference Planning Committee

FEBRUARY 12 MEETING LOCATION

The 10 a.m. February 12 meeting of the Conference Planning Committee will be held in suite 101 at the Willowbrook Inn on Route 17. An agenda with full meeting details is enclosed.

The Willowbrook is a new facility about two miles west of town. If you are not familiar with its location, I suggest you follow these directions from the downtown area:

1. Pick up Interstate 76 south off Branson parkway or off north 83rd Street.
2. Follow 76 south to the Route 11 exit about 3 miles from center city.
3. Take Route 11 west one-half mile and turn right onto Route 17 north. The Willowbrook is a quarter mile down the road on the left.

If you have any questions, please call my secretary at 202-1117 (I'll be away until February 9).

WRITING REPORTS

Many reports--both internal and external--are prepared in the memo format. Models 13.34 and 13.36 through 13.38 are examples of informal memo reports. Model 13.35 is an example of a report transmittal memo. See chapter 16 for models of pages from a formal report.

The Short, Informal Report

13.34. Status Report

TO: Wendall Morris

DAVIS RECLAMATION PROJECT STATUS REPORT

We have almost reached the midway point in our reclamation project at Wintergreen Acres. The following steps have been completed:

Step 1: Surveying

Step 2: Removal of dead trees and underbrush

Step 3: Drainage of pond and associated swampland

Step 4: Burning off of remaining dead growth (anything presenting a fire hazard)

The following steps have been approved and funded and will be undertaken during August and September:

Step 5: Clearing four-acre site for the Wintergreen cottages

Step 6: Resoding public lawn area (2.5 acres)

Step 7: Planting fringe and park trees and shrubs

Our estimated completion date is September 25. No cost variations from our original estimate are evident at this time.

The next status report will be sent to you on August 15. In the meantime, if you have any questions just let me know.

Transmittal Memo for Formal Report

13.35. To All Departments

TO: Department Mangers

QUARTERLY REPORT

A copy of our report on sales activity during the first quarter of this year is enclosed for your review. I would like to call your attention to two items that will be discussed at the next meeting of all departmental heads:

1. Although the figure for quantities of machines shipped suggests an increase during this period over the previous quarter, there was actually a substantial decline in shipments compared with this same period last year (see page 7 of the report).

2. The closing of our Houston operation has created a serious bottleneck at our Kansas City plant (see page 11 of the report).

You will have an opportunity to comment on these problems and other matters in the report at the next meeting. Until then, I'll be glad to hear from you if you have any questions.

Credit Report

13.36. On Customer

TO: Credit Department

CREDIT REPORT: PELLITIER STUDIOS

Our records indicate that Pellitier Studios has an excellent credit standing with our company. They have maintained an account with us since 1975, with purchases averaging $350 monthly.

Our experience suggests that you would be justified in extending a reasonable amount of credit to Pellitier Studios.

If I can offer any further information, do let me know.

Informal Meeting Notes

13.37. On Committee Meeting

TO: Warren Ricotti

PUBLICITY COMMITTEE: DECEMBER MEETING

While waiting for the official minutes of the December 5 Publicity Committee meeting, you may want to review the key points we covered.

1. Miles Bradstreet will resign as chair, effective February 1. We should elect a new chair at the January 14 meeting.

2. Publicity for the Lawrenceville Arts and Crafts Festival on March 19 is underway. First press release was mailed December 7.

3. A copy of next year's budget will be mailed with the December meeting minutes. Discussion and approval to be on the January meeting agenda.

4. Tom Wilson proposed that we hold open house in July next year instead of June to take advantage of the heavier tourist traffic. Discussion slated for the January meeting.

After we receive the official minutes, I'll contact you to discuss some of these matters before the January meeting. If you have any questions before then, Warren, just give me a call.

Proposal Report

13.38. Mailing List

TO: Edward Morhardt

PROPOSAL TO IMPROVE MAIL DELIVERABILITY

Our returns of undeliverable mail have been ranging from 20 to 35 percent this year. This figure suggests not only an ongoing nuisance to the mailroom but also lost sales and unproductive mailing costs. The best avenue available to improve mail deliverability, and hence to recapture lost sales, is the National Change of Address (NCOA) file of the U.S. Postal Service.

WHAT THE NCOA FILE DOES

The NCOA file rapidly updates old mailing lists by matching them with information provided by 211 Computer Forwarding System sites.

BENEFITS OF NCOA

In addition to gaining accurate addresses, mailers can qualify for automation discounts by running a list through the NCOA file. Having current addresses permits a more timely mail delivery and reduces multiple handling delays of mail forwarding.

COST OF NCOA

Although NCOA was designed for large lists maintained on magnetic tape or cartridge, mailers with smaller lists maintained on diskette can also use NCOA. The charge for diskette coding is $7 per thousand addresses, with a minimum charge of $25. There is no charge for lists containing more than 3,600 addresses.

FURTHER INFORMATION

The National Address Information Center (NAIC) in Memphis will provide a list of NCOA licensees, an application for diskette NCOA coding, and other information. The toll-free NAIC number is 1-800-238-3150.

CONCLUSION

This preliminary information suggests that the cost of NCOA updating for one list would be far less than the present cost of undeliverable mail. Therefore, I believe we should contact a representative of NAIC and make arrangements to apply for diskette NCOA coding. If you agree, I would be happy to follow through on this proposed mailing-list update.

SENDING CONFIRMATIONS

Confirmations of routine matters—scheduled meetings, receipts, and so on—can frequently be prepared in memo format. If numerous notices with the same general information must be sent (such as confirming meeting registrations), the confirmations may be prepared by computer or prepared as preprinted forms, with only the pertinent facts filled in individually for each recipient. In any case, the confirmation must provide all necessary data, clearly and accurately, and it must be sent in time for the recipient to act or respond as required.

Meeting Details

13.39. Staff Meeting

TO: All Staff Members

APRIL 4 STAFF MEETING

This will confirm that the next staff meeting will be held on Thursday, April 4, at 9:30 a.m., in Bob Cramer's office. Please let me know right away if you will be unable to attend.

Thanks very much.

Conference Registration

13.40. Annual Conference

TO: Marlene Singleton

CONSERVATIONIST SOCIETY ANNUAL CONFERENCE

We are happy to confirm your preliminary registration for the Fourth Annual Conference of the Conservationist Society, May 14-15, at the Civic Center in Provo, Utah.

To complete your registration, a conference fee of $65 is payable by May 1. Please make your check payable to the Conservationist Society and mail it to the society office at 114 Pine Grove, Logan, UT 84322.

Thank you.

Information: Payment Received

13.41. For Conference Proceedings

TO: Paul Fryatt

TWENTY-SECOND PROCEEDINGS

We have received your check for $37.95 for one copy of our Twenty-second Annual Conference Proceedings, The New Medical Frontiers. Thank you very much.

As you requested, rather than mail the book to you, Mr. Adams will personally take it along to your meeting with him on Saturday evening, August 17.

Order Received

13.42. For Survey Details

TO: Betty McKinsey

MEMBERSHIP SURVEY

Thank you for your order for a copy of our recent membership survey report. There has been a slight delay in production, but the reports will be ready in two weeks, and your copy will be sent promptly at that time.

Project Approval

13.43. Conference Exhibit

TO: Barry Attleboro

Thank you for approving our request to have a literature booth at the National Manufacturer's Tenth Annual Conference. We will follow the plan sent to you on September 6 and next week will send you a final list of display materials for your approval.

WRITING TRANSMITTAL MEMOS

Transmittal correspondence is often a very simple type of communication: brief and factual. Thus the memo format is ideal for many transmittal communications, and models 13.44 through 13.47 are examples of the type of transmittal correspondence suitable for the memo format. See also model 13.35 for an example of a report transmittal memo.

Company Literature

13.44. To Prospective Customer

TO: Monte Evans

SARTWELL'S CUSTOM LAB SERVICE

Here is the literature you requested on the Sartwell Company and our Custom Lab Service. The enclosed brochure explains in detail our various techniques and procedures for placing orders.

We very much appreciate your interest and hope you will let us know if we can be of service.

Company Product

13.45. To Customer

TO: David Lewis

CENTURY 2000 GAS WELDER

Here, hot off the press, are the new specs on our Century 2000 Gas Welder. I'll have more details on the welder when I see you next week, Dave.

For Material-Information Requested

13.46. Company Department

TO: Diane Warnecki

MASKING FILM

Enclosed are the four rolls of .003" Rubylith film you ordered for your Art Department.

We also have the .003" Amberlith film that you asked about in pads of ten sheets each: 8 1/2 x 11 ($15/pad) and 11 x 14 ($18.50/pad).

If we can be of further help, please do let us know. We appreciate your interest in our products.

Remittance

13.47. For Book Sales

TO: Creighton's Book Store

BOOK ORDER

Enclosed is our check for $234.90 along with a completed book sale order form. If any of the books are not available, we would appreciate receiving an immediate refund rather than credit on future purchases.

Thank you.

14

Memos That Make a Request

LIKE the memo that *gives* information (chapter 13), the memo that *requests* something was formerly used primarily in internal communication. Now it is also used for external contacts. In both internal and external correspondence, the memo format is ideal for rapid communication, and in many offices the memo is used as an economy measure since it usually takes less time to prepare than a formal letter and, if desired, can be prepared on less expensive paper than formal letterhead stationery (see chapter 19).

Memos that request something, like those that give information, are usually factual and concise and follow a specific pattern. Store them in your computer file so that you can recall them for future use.

You will write and send many of the memos in this chapter (such as 14.4). Others (such as 14.7) you may draft for your boss. Occasionally, your boss may prefer to draft the memo (such 14.33) but will expect you to polish and refine it. (See chapter 1 for requests handled by letter and consult the Model Selector Guide for models of other requests throughout the book.)

All requests, whether made by memo or letter, should be specific and clear.

1. Tell what you want (possibly why you want it).

2. Explain what action you want the reader to take.

3. Specify all pertinent facts, such as time, place, price, delivery.

4. Express appreciation if a favor or special effort is required.

Thirty-eight models are illustrated in the following nine categories: requests for help (14.1–14.5), surveys (14.6–14.8), follow-up inquiries (14.9–14.12), information for reports (14.13–14.17), personal or professional information (14.18–14.22), product-service information (14.23–14.28), literature requests (14.29–14.32), action requests (14.33–14.35), and solicitations for contributions (14.36–14.38). Although the basic purpose of these memos is to *ask* for something, they may, in the process, also *give* information.

ASKING FOR HELP

Examples of assistance needed in a business office are endless, but all situations share common features. The right person must be contacted, the need for help must be explained, and pertinent details—when, where, and so on—must be given. Models 14.1 through 14.5 illustrate the types of requests for help that are suitable for the memo format.

Temporary Office Assistance

14.1. For Secretary

TO: Joan Florette

TEMPORARY CLERICAL HELP

I'm in need of temporary clerical assistance for my secretary, Margie Woodward. Since we're in the midst of our annual sales campaign, Margie's work load has increased substantially, and her usual duties are suffering as a result.

I'd like to have someone from the word processing pool or from the Mail Department assist us during the next two weeks--through Friday, May 5. Our principal needs are (1) addressing envelopes and (2) folding inserts and stuffing and sealing envelopes.

Anything you can do to help will be much appreciated, Joan. Thanks very much.

Special Work Project

14.2. *For Department*

TO: Scott Aldrich

LIST CONVERSION

Would it be possible for your assistant, Bob Watts, to spend a couple of days next week helping us check over the Public Relations Department's mailing list?

We're converting the list from metal plates to computer and want to go through the Southwest section, which hasn't been checked for at least five years. Since Bob is more familiar with the names in this section than anyone in our department, it would be helpful if he could assist us in selecting rejects.

Please give me a call if you can spare him on Monday and Tuesday next week. I'd really appreciate it, Scott. Thanks very much.

Permanent Committee

14.3. *For Club*

TO: Rita Farnsworth

BUSINESS WOMEN'S CLUB ENTERTAINMENT COMMITTEE

Our Entertainment Committee cochair recently informed me that her committee lost two members and is in need of assistance to complete the entertainment plans for our August and October dinner meetings and for our December Christmas party. Since all of the regular programs seem to be fairly well established and some of your Program Committee members will be without assignments most of the year, I was wondering if anyone on your committee could transfer to the Entertainment Committee on a permanent basis.

If this sounds feasible to you, I'd appreciate it if you would let me know right away. Thanks very much, Rita.

Planning a Company Event

14.4. Picnic

TO: Ben Byse

AUGUST 11 COMPANY PICNIC: TRANSPORTATION

Our office is in charge of planning for the company picnic on August 11, so I'm contacting a number of persons who might be able to help us with arrangements. Since you're in charge of the motor pool, I was wondering if you could make arrangements for transportation from the company to Carnegie Lake and back again on the day of the picnic.

We will need enough cars and drivers for about fifty employees and guests. The cars should leave from the motor pool entrance at noon and return from the Carnegie Lodge entrance at 4 o'clock.

I'd very much appreciate your help in making these arrangements. Please let me know right away if we can count on you for our transportation needs on August 11. Thanks, Ben.

To Solve a Problem

14.5. In Meeting a Deadline

TO: Nancy Almond

MANAGEMENT NEWSLETTER

Would you be able to submit your marketing report for our April issue of Management News one week early this month--by Friday, March 23? Since I'll be away during the regularly scheduled week of production, I'll have to submit all copy in advance to meet our deadline.

Let me know if you can manage an early report. Your help will be greatly appreciated. Thanks very much, Nancy.

CONDUCTING SURVEYS

The memo format is often ideal for conducting surveys. Sometimes the questions to be asked can be incorporated into the body of the memo; at other times it is more practical to use the memo for transmittal information and enclose a separate questionnaire.

Models 14.6 through 14.8 illustrate different ways that the memos can be used in surveys.

To Estimate Attendance

14.6. At Meeting

TO: Members of the Community Service Association

ANNUAL MEETING

The Program Committee is making arrangements for the October 15 annual meeting of the Community Service Association at the Lakeville Civic Center. (A program was sent to you earlier this month.) To help us make adequate room and luncheon reservations, we would appreciate knowing whether you plan to attend this meeting.

For your convenience, space is provided below for you to indicate your intention. Please return this memo in the enclosed postage-paid envelope by September 5. Thank you.

( ) Yes, I will attend.   ( ) No, I will be unable to attend.

_____
Signature

To Determine Interest

14.7. In Seminar

TO: Joan Ricardo

RECRUITMENT SEMINAR

A bulletin is enclosed describing a one-day recruitment seminar for admissions personnel. The program is scheduled for April 9 at the Holiday Inn in Dumont.

I'd appreciate knowing whether you believe any of the Admissions Office personnel should attend this seminar. If you think it would be worthwhile, Joan, let me know, and we can discuss arrangements for registrations and transportation.

To Update Records

14.8. Personnel Data

TO: Department Heads

PERSONNEL RECORDS

Periodically, we need to review and update our personnel records at the Oxford Company so that they will be as current and accurate as possible. Nonconfidential information (marriages, prizes, and so on) is used by our publicity department in preparing news releases and by our executive board in selecting recipients for special recognition and commendation.

I'm enclosing a supply of one-page questionnaires to be completed by all employees in your department. (If you need more forms, let me know.) I'd appreciate it if you would distribute and collect these forms and return them to me by January 1.

Thanks very much for your help and cooperation.

SENDING FOLLOW-UP INQUIRIES

Although the letter format is often used for follow-ups (see chapter 4), there are many occasions when follow-up inquiries can be made by memo. Some of these inquiries are routine follow-ups concerning factual data about shipments, appointments, and so on. Models 14.9 through 14.12 are examples of follow-up inquiries prepared in the memo format.

For Meeting Details

14.9. About the Agenda

TO: Dave Montgomery

EXECUTIVE COMMITTEE MEETING AGENDA

The agenda for our June 4 Executive Committee meeting is almost ready. All I need are final details from you on the construction plans. Have you had an opportunity to confirm the Fraser Construction bid we discussed last week?

I'd appreciate it if you would let me know by Friday whether the bid is firm. Thanks, Dave.

Date of Shipment

14.10. Of Order

TO: All-Season Greenery

ORDER 06102

On March 11 we placed an order for eleven large floor plants to be shipped from your greenhouse to Martek Engineering at 421 North Fordham Street in Brockton. A copy of our order number 06102 is enclosed.

Would you please let us know the date of shipment and anticipated delivery date to our offices? We are expecting out-of-town clients to arrive on April 17 and want to be certain that the plants will be here before that date.

Thank you.

About Appointment

14.11. Tentative Date

TO: Harold Crosby

BUILDING INSPECTION

I was wondering if you're in a position yet to confirm our tentative date to inspect the vacant building at 11 Waterfront Avenue next week. There's a note on my calendar to meet you on-site at 3 o'clock on October 5.

I'd appreciate a call as soon as you know if you can make it. Thanks very much, Hal.

For Further Information

14.12. On Product

TO: Art Supplies, Inc.

DRAFTING TABLES

Thank you for sending a copy of your general catalog. The equipment section has four light tables, each available in three sizes. We are particularly interested in one of the large floor models, number 1250, and would like to receive more information about this table.

Please send full specifications and an order form to Jarred Phillips, manager, Burr and Hodges, Communications Consultants, Highway 51, Columbia, MO 65201. Thank you.

REQUESTING AND ACKNOWLEDGING INFORMATION FOR REPORTS

Reports are based on information that often must be collected from various sources. The written request for this information can be handled in a number of ways: letter, form, or memo. Routine communications are frequently well suited for the memo format, as models 14.13 through 14.17 illustrate.

General Guidance Information

14.13. From Research Department

TO: Margaret Eddington

REPORT: USE OF PLASTICS IN APPLIANCE MANUFACTURE

Joel Steinberg is preparing a report on the use of plastics in the manufacture of household appliances. He was wondering if your department has compiled any information in this area that might be helpful.

Specifically, Mr. Steinberg is concerned with the effect of plastics on life expectancy of appliances. For instance, many vacuum cleaner manufacturers are now using more plastic and less metal in their products: How has this reduced life expectancy or otherwise contributed to replacement and repair needs?

I know that Mr. Steinberg would greatly appreciate any information you have on the use of plastics in appliance manufacture. Thank you very much for your help.

Statistical Information

14.14. From Accounting Department

TO: Shaun Fenton

PAYROLL DATA FOR REPORT

Elizabeth Damione is preparing a five-year review of staff salaries for the general manager and would like to know if you have payroll data that would be pertinent to her study. She will be looking for general patterns in salary changes and specific patterns related to job level.

Would you please let Ms. Damione know sometime next week whether you have payroll data that she might find helpful? Thank you very much.

Permission to Quote: Extract

14.15. *From Publisher*

TO: Permissions Editor

PERMISSION TO USE MATERIAL FROM COMPUTER STUDIES

We are preparing an article for the August issue of our association newsletter, Computer Briefs. May we have your permission to include the description of "debugging" on page 411 of Computer Studies, by Mark Cromwell (1992)? A photocopy of the section we would like to use is enclosed.

For your convenience, a form is provided below to grant your permission and to indicate your preferred credit line.

Your consent will be greatly appreciated. Thank you very much.

CREDIT LINE:

_____

_____

_____

I (we) grant permission for the use requested above.

_____   _____
Signature   Date

Credit Information

14.16. *On Distributor*

TO: Credit Department

REFERENCES FOR SMITH AND HARRIS, INC.

Smith and Harris, Inc., a local distributor of automotive parts and accessories, has filed a request with us to purchase goods on account at our usual terms. According to their application, you have extended credit to them on previous occasions.

We would appreciate knowing something about your experience with Smith and Harris. Your comments will be held in the strictest confidence.

Thank you very much.

Thank You

14.17. Information Received

TO: Dana Perone

NBP LASER PRINTER

I just read your detailed comments on the NBP laser printer. This is just what I need to complete my report on miniprinters, and I really appreciate your efforts in rushing the information to me.

Sincerest thanks, Dana, for all your help.

SOLICITING PERSONAL AND PROFESSIONAL INFORMATION

Businesses frequently use personal as well as professional information about employees in preparing publicity releases, in evaluating candidates for awards and promotions, and in making suitable work assignments. Such information could be collected by letter, form, or memo. Sometimes a memo serves primarily as a transmittal communication, with the information request prepared as an attachment such as a questionnaire form. Models 14.18 through 14.22 illustrate how this information is requested in the memo format.

For a News Release

14.18. About Branch Manager

TO: Stephen Libby

DATA FOR NEWS RELEASE

We're preparing a release on your upcoming transfer to our Denver office. To be certain that we have our facts correct, I'd appreciate it if you would complete the attached personal data sheet and return it to me by November 1.

Thanks very much, Steve.

For Company Records

14.19. For Public Relations Office

TO: Charles Wright

EXECUTIVE DATA FILE

We're updating our executive data files and would appreciate your help in bringing our records up to date. These files are used by our writers in preparing press releases and newsletter announcements that concern company executives.

To simplify matters, I'm enclosing your complete file for you to review, along with a new data sheet for you to complete. If you spot anything in the file that's out of date, please attach an updated replacement. For instance, should the photographs of you be replaced with something more current?

I'd like to have the updated file back by December 1. In the meantime, if you have any questions, just let me know. Thanks very much for your help and cooperation, Mr. Wright.

To Make Work-Committee Assignments

14.20. To Staff

TO: Donna Margolis

COMMITTEE STAFF ASSIGNMENTS

I'm enclosing a list of newly elected chairs for our Budget, Social Relations, and Training committees. These chairs will soon be calling on us to provide staff assistance during the coming year.

Last year we provided assistance on a random basis to whoever was free at the time a task was presented. This year I would like to try a more organized approach. Let's select six persons from our staff in advance, two for each committee. The same individuals, then, will assist the same committee throughout the year. This consistency and their growing familiarity with the work and the committee's needs should make everyone's job easier.

To help me make appropriate assignments, I'd appreciate it if you would have each person in our office complete the enclosed biographical fact sheets. Any recommendations you have will also be welcome. As soon as I have the assignments ready, I'll forward the information to you.

If you have any questions, Donna, let me know. Many thanks for your help.

On Job Applicant

14.21. Reference Request

TO: David K. Ascott

ARTHUR LATTIMER

We have received your name as a reference for Arthur Lattimer, who has applied for the position of assistant production supervisor with our firm.

Any information you can provide that will help us evaluate this candidate's training, professional background, job skills, and performance record will be greatly appreciated. Your comments will be held in the strictest confidence.

Enclosed is a self-addressed, stamped envelope for your reply. Thank you.

For Employee Recognition

14.22. Awards Night

TO: Sam Sorensen

PERSONAL DATA FOR AWARDS INTRODUCTION

Henry Barkley is preparing his presentation speech for the award you are to receive on June 11 and would like to have more background information about you. Would you please complete the enclosed biographical data sheet and return it to Mr. Barkley by June 5?

Thank you very much.

REQUESTING PRODUCT-SERVICE INFORMATION

Most requests for information about products and services are ideally suited to the memo format. Such requests may involve external as well as internal communications as illustrated in models 14.23 through 14.28. Frequently, these requests are just directed to a company rather than to a specific individual, or they may be addressed to a department such as the Service Department or Sales Department.

Inquiry About Service

14.23. For Pickup and Delivery

TO: Rossetti's Uniform Pressing and Cleaning Service

SCHEDULE AND RATES

A recent newspaper advertisement indicates that you are now providing pickup and delivery service in East Lansing. Please send us a schedule of rates with hours and days when you would be able to pick up and deliver fifty uniforms at Jones Tool and Die Works, 1450 Juniper Lane, in East Lansing.

Thank you.

Inquiry About Equipment

14.24. For Maintenance

TO: Bromley's Office Equipment Center

MAINTENANCE CONTRACT FOR DICTATING EQUIPMENT

Several months ago we purchased three Starlite model 50 dictation and transcription units from you. Now that the warranties have expired we would like to have the units covered by a maintenance service agreement. Please have one of your representatives call on us within the next two weeks or send us full details on your contracts by mail.

Thank you.

Price and Delivery Details

14.25. On Office Equipment

TO: Major Office Suppliers, Inc.

PAPER SHREDDERS

Please send us information, including price, warranty, and delivery details, on your paper shredders. We are primarily interested in models that will adjust to fit any standard wastebasket and that have automatic start and stop features.

Thank you.

For Further Information

14.26. On New Equipment

TO: The Complete Entertainment Center

COMPUTERIZED TV CONVERTER

Thank you for sending a brochure describing your new minicomputer TV converter with snap-in cartridges. Since we would be interested in a number of these units, we were wondering if multiple TV adaptors are available for plug-in operation on several sets.

Any further information that you can provide on multiple use will be very much appreciated. Thank you.

Cost Estimate

14.27. Request for Bid

TO: Hudson Factory Outlet, Inc.

REQUEST FOR PRICE QUOTATION

We are soliciting price quotations on mobile panel systems for private workstations, including the following features:

T-base feet

Connector kits to join up to four panels

60" W x 72" H

Sound-resistant beige or gray fabric boards

We will require a complex suitable for twelve workstations. Please return your specifications and quotation, including installation costs, to the attention of Andrea T. Arnette, Room 1072. Thank you.

Invoice

14.28. Request for Billing

TO: Accounting Department

REQUEST FOR INVOICE

Five months ago, on October 14, your firm supplied us with recessed fixtures and wiring for a one-room addition to our chemical laboratory at 421 31st Street in Dayton. Our records indicate that we never received an invoice from you, and we would like to complete our financial statements for this project. May we, therefore, have a final bill from you for this project?

Thank you.

REQUESTING LITERATURE

Businesses and other organizations must constantly request literature of all sorts: product and service brochures, reports, travel information, educational literature, and so on. Such material is frequently requested by letter, but a routine literature request is also suitable for the memo format. Models 14.29 through 14.32 illustrate several types of brief, straightforward requests for literature that can be made by memo.

Product Brochure

14.29. For Manager

TO: The Pro Camera Shop

160 PRO CAMCORDER

Please send a brochure on your new AL 160 Pro Camcorder to David Collins, manager, Hartz Custom Studios, P.O. Box 100, Dallas, TX 75221. Thank you.

Reports and Studies

14.30. For the Library

TO: The Wheeler Technical Institute

INDEX TO REPORTS AND STUDIES

Please send an index to your reports and studies, along with a current price list and order form, to the attention of Marlene Baker, librarian.

Thank you.

Meeting Notes

14.31. For Reference

TO: Joe Cossetti

MARCH 9 EXECUTIVE COMMITTEE MEETING NOTES

Since the minutes of our March 9 meeting won't be available for several weeks, I'd appreciate having a copy of your meeting notes for temporary reference. Thanks, Joe.

Travel Literature

14.32. For Upcoming Trip

TO: Sue Johnston

INFORMATION FOR TRIP TO ENGLAND

Estelle Hoffman would like to arrange a trip to England--leaving New York September 1 and returning September 22--and would like to see some literature on two- and three-day excursions from her base in London. She will attend meetings in London on September 5, 12, and 16 but would like to travel and sightsee the rest of the time.

Any descriptive literature you have on sightseeing opportunities suitable for her schedule will be very much appreciated.

Thanks very much, Sue.

REQUESTING ACTION

Communications that ask someone to take action are often sent by letter (see chapter 1) but in certain instances are also suitable for the memo format. Models 14.33 through 14.35 depict this type of action request.

Budget Approval

14.33. For Department

TO: Jim Stockton

APPROVAL OF ADVERTISING DEPARTMENT BUDGET

I'm enclosing a copy of our proposed departmental budget for the coming fiscal year. The figures are essentially those you gave me with only three minor refinements, which I've marked in red. If you'll approve the budget, I'll submit it to the Finance Committee right away.

Thanks very much, Mr. Stockton.

Change in Procedure

14.34. For Staff

TO: Training Department Staff

SUPPLIES

To help the Supply Office streamline its operations, the training director has asked us to employ better control measures in ordering supplies for our department. The procedure has been for each person to go to the Supply Office independently and select whatever he or she needs at the time. The new procedure, effective immediately, will be for each person to fill out a requisition form in my office, ask the director to initial it, and then take the form to the Supply Office.

I know the director will appreciate your help and cooperation in improving our procedure in this area. Thanks very much.

Job Assignment

14.35. Request for Additional Duties

TO: Adam Goldman

FORMS FILE

As you know, Mr. Goldman, the various offices in our company maintain their own data files, including, when appropriate, their own forms files. Some are computerized, and some are traditional hard-copy files. During the past year I've discovered a tremendous amount of duplication of effort because of this decentralized policy.

Would it be possible for me to assume responsibility for establishing and maintaining a centralized electronic forms file, one that is accessible to all offices? Since our department uses so many forms, it would save me a lot of time otherwise spent in contacting the other offices for permission to examine and use forms from their files and would help everyone throughout the firm in that a larger stock would be open to all personnel.

I realize that the initial task of merging a dozen different files into one would be time consuming, but after that, I expect the maintenance function to involve minimal effort on my part and would not interfere with my other work.

I hope you agree that this would be a worthwhile extension of my duties, and I'll look forward to learning your decision. Thank you.

SOLICITING CONTRIBUTIONS

Many organizations have a standard procedure for collecting contributions to charities or for special events. Depending on the size of the organization and the number of people to be reached, the procedure may involve personal contact or some type of mailing. Sometimes envelopes are circulated with printed instructions, and sometimes letters or memos accompany the envelopes. Models 14.36 through 14.38 are examples of several types of solicitations that could be handled by memo.

Company Picnic Donations

14.36. From All Employees

TO: All Employees

COMPANY PICNIC CONTRIBUTIONS FOR ORPHANS

This year, Harris Manufacturing Company will entertain children from the Pine Grove Orphanage at its August 14 company picnic in Kennedy Park. The company will provide transportation and lunch for all children plus admission to the entertainment facilities at the park.

Many of us at Harris want to do one other thing--have a grabbag of gifts so that each child will receive one small present. The Personnel Office has volunteered to select the gifts and make arrangements for the grabbag distribution. It is up to us now to contribute generously to a fund to support this effort.

Please place your donation in the enclosed envelope and return it to the Personnel Office by August 1. Thank you very much for helping to make this worthwhile effort possible.

Employee Recognition Fund

14.37. From Department Staff

TO: Staff Members

EMPLOYEE RECOGNITION FUND

Two years ago, by unanimous agreement, we established the Employee Recognition Fund to finance an annual award to the employee who made the greatest contribution to successful departmental operations during the year. Once again, it is time to honor one of our staff at the annual departmental banquet on December 13.

The fund, as you know, is supported by our own donations. Therefore, I'm enclosing an envelope for you to use this year in making the contribution of your choice. Please return the envelope to me by November 15.

Thanks very much for your continuing support and generosity.

For Charitable Organization

14.38. From Business Associate

TO: Bill Jamison

ANNUAL CHARITY DRIVE

I've been asked by the United Community Drive to encourage the support of executives in our company this year for this worthwhile cause.

Funds collected by the United Community Drive go to all needy organizations in our community. Donations, however, may be earmarked for a particular need such as the Lowrey Home for Underprivileged Children or the new Cancer Treatment Center at the hospital. Without a successful drive, many of these vital organizations would have to reduce their services, and some that are struggling just to exist might even have to close their doors.

I'm convinced that the need is real and important, and I plan to make a generous contribution this year. I sincerely hope that you can do the same. Just make your check payable to the United Community Drive and mail it to P.O. Box 40 here in Evanston.

Thanks for your help, Bill.

Part

III

OTHER MESSAGES

15

Announcements

and Invitations

SUCCESSFUL businesses cannot neglect the social side of their operations. Invitations and announcements are issued for a variety of events, such as a luncheon, a dinner party, a reception, an open house, and an exhibition. These occasions are used to enhance the company image, to build better relations with clients and customers, and often to conduct business or at least to pave the way for a later transaction. A secretary must be familiar with the style and format of the various business announcements and invitations. Personal secretaries may also be expected to handle their boss's nonbusiness social invitations and replies.

Although informal announcements and invitations (see chapter 9) are usually prepared by typewriter or computer in a business-letter format, formal announcements and invitations are printed on special paper or card stock and are usually ordered from printers or stationery/office-supply stores. These suppliers have books of samples in both modern and traditional styles. Which style is most appropriate depends on the image your employer wants to convey. An open-house announcement for a toy store would likely be modern and innovative whereas an announcement for a law firm would no doubt be dignified and conservative. Ask your boss if you have any doubts. Also, check the files for examples of previous announcements and invitations used by your firm or your boss.

MAKING ANNOUNCEMENTS

Models 15.1 through 15.4 illustrate a common format and wording for various types of announcements that you may be asked to order. These announcements usually would be ordered through a printer or a stationery/office-supply store.

Formal Announcement: Business

15.1. Office Opening

Lee W. Webster, CPA

announces the opening of his office

for the practice of accounting

at

4310 Marmont Circle

Peoria, Illinois 61605

309-272-9100

Formal Announcement: Individual

15.2. Promotion

Adams Milling, Incorporated

is pleased to announce the appointment of

Darwin Polette

as

general manager

October 19--

851 Jackson Heights

Baton Rouge, Louisiana 70810

504-617-3000

Informal Announcement: Business

15.3. New Store

Wyatt Selig

has opened a new store

Southwestern Furniture and Accessories

and wants to welcome his friends to

One Forest Boulevard

Glendale, Arizona 85308

602-734-1906

Informal Announcement: Individual

15.4. Change of Address

Elizabeth Courtney

(formerly Elizabeth Courtney-Schoenfeld)

has changed her address to

2100 Olson Lane

East Orange, NJ 07017

SENDING AND ACKNOWLEDGING
FORMAL INVITATIONS

Models 15.5 through 15.7 are examples of traditional formal invitations that are commonly ordered through printers or stationery/office-supply stores. Sometimes the invitation is partially printed or engraved and the pertinent facts are filled in later in ink (see model 15.7).

Models 15.8 through 15.11 illustrate the proper format for formal replies. Whether the reply is typed or handwritten (nonbusiness, social replies should always be handwritten), the reply is worded in the third person using the same format as that given on the invitation. Personal stationery, which is smaller than 8 1/2-by-11-inch business letterhead, is used, either plain or with the sender's name or monogram on it.

Formal Invitation: Business

15.5. Company Anniversary

SAMWORTH TEMPORARY OFFICE SERVICES

Brandon Kearney III
President and General Manager
cordially invites you to
cocktails
to celebrate the company's tenth year of service
Friday, November 16
5 to 7 p.m.
3214 Deever Street
Fayetteville

R.s.v.p. card enclosed

Formal Invitation: Individual

15.6. Dinner

Julia Glidden Fairwood
requests the pleasure of your company
at dinner
on Saturday, the twentieth of June
at half past seven o'clock
202 LaCrosse Street
Rome, Georgia 30161
404-588-6837

R.s.v.p

Formal Fill-in Invitation

15.7. Dinner

(logo)

Mr. and Mrs. Roger Sessler
request the pleasure of your company

at *dinner*

on *Friday, the fourth of May*

at *half after eight o'clock*

19 Minton Avenue
Fort Worth

R.s.v.p.
321-8050

Reply to Formal Invitation: Acceptance

15.8. Lunch

Mr. David Monroe
accepts with pleasure
Mr. and Mrs. Landers'
kind invitation for
Tuesday, the ninth of August
at one o'clock

Reply to Formal Invitation: Regret

15.9. Reception

Miss Joreen Erickson

regrets that she is unable to accept

the kind invitation of

Mr. and Mrs. William Tye

for Saturday, the sixth of February

at five o'clock

Reply to Formal Invitation: Combination

15.10. Dinner-Dance

Mr. Daniel Cramer

accepts with pleasure

Miss Michelle Mercedes-Stowe's

kind invitation for

Friday, the fourth of December

at half past seven o'clock

but regrets that

Mrs. Cramer

will be unable to attend

Reply to Formal Invitation: R.s.v.p. Card

15.11. Dinner

(logo)

Mr. *Dale Foredell*

Name of Guest *Sharon Obsidian*

Accept ✓ Regret ___ Tel. No. _____

Dinner, April 12th at 7:30 p.m.
Hillside Bar and Grill
36 Signpost Courtyard
Salt Lake City, Utah

SENDING AND ACKNOWLEDGING
INFORMAL INVITATIONS

Informal invitations and replies may be made by letter (see chapter 9) or by using one of the informal card formats, such as a fill-in card (15.12) or a foldover card (15.13–15.14), all of which can be purchased in stationery stores and many office-supply stores.

Informal Invitation: Fill-in

15.12. Party

YOU'RE INVITED!

to _a Thanksgiving party_
on _Thursday the 26th, 2 o'clock_
at _Heartline Restaurant, 13 Eighth Ave._
Reply to _461-5872 (Doris)_

Informal Invitation: Foldover Card

15.13. Cocktails

Cocktails

Mr. and Mrs. Bernard Sloane

Saturday, May 5th
6 o'clock
22 Orange Street

Regrets only
512-9237

Reply to Informal Invitation: Foldover Card

15.14. Acceptance

accept with pleasure
Saturday at 8:00

Jim and Cindy Olivet

16

Reports and Press Releases

BUSINESSES, professional organizations, and various institutions use different formats to report facts and figures both to associates within the organization and to outside clients and customers. Most reports, particularly in-house communications, are brief and can easily be prepared in a memo or letter format (see chapter 13). But other reports that are long and complex require a more formal presentation.

It will be your responsibility to see that the different parts of a report are properly styled and formatted. To save time in the future, store the models in this chapter in your computer for recall later. Although the data will be different in each report, the format specifications can be repeated in each new document.

A formal report is usually prepared on 8 1/2-by-11-inch typewriter or computer paper. Large companies with desktop or other publishing capability may also prepare long formal reports as bound books. Short typewriter or computer-prepared reports are often double-spaced whereas long documents are frequently single-spaced.

A formal report will have some or all of these parts: title page (16.1), authorization letter or memo (16.2), transmittal letter (16.3), table of contents (16.4), summary or abstract (16.5), acknowledgments (16.6), body (16.7-16.8), appendix (16.9-16.10), references (16.11), and glossary (16.12).

The press release is a different type of vehicle that conveys information. It is sent to newspapers, magazines, and other media when an organization wants to make a newsworthy announcement.

Press release messages must be factual and avoid subjective adjectives such as *tremendous* or *wonderful.*

Press releases are usually typed or printed out double-spaced on special release letterhead or on regular business letterhead. Sometimes press releases are published as written; sometimes they are rewritten entirely. Since you want to capture the editor's attention and because editors tend to delete paragraphs from the end when there isn't room to carry the entire message, the sender should be certain that paragraphs are presented in the order of importance. Models 16.13 and 16.14 illustrate an acceptable format for business press releases.

PREPARING REPORTS

The models presented below (16.1-16.12) illustrate twelve familiar parts in a long formal report. Although many of these models are shown in a double-spaced format (16.5-16.12), you could also prepare them single-spaced, particularly if your report is long.

Formal Report

16.1. Title Page

INTEREST-CAPITALIZATION TAX GUIDE

Prepared for

Marilyn J. Sutter, Manager
Creative Plastics, Inc.
270 West End Avenue, N.E.
Washington, D.C. 20260

Prepared by

Carl P. Darrell, CPA
National Accounting Services
1059 20th Street, N.E.
Washington, D.C. 20260

November 16, 19--

16.2. Authorization Letter

[Letterhead]

DATE: September 15, 19--

TO: Carl P. Darrell, CPA

FROM: Vincent Truesdale, General Manager

INTEREST-CAPITALIZATION TAX GUIDE

This will authorize you to prepare an interest-capitalization tax guide report for Marilyn J. Sutter, manager, Creative Plastics, Inc., 270 West End Avenue, N.E., Washington, D.C. 20260.

Creative Plastics' request for a report (September 12: copy enclosed) explains the company's need for specific tax guidelines concerning the (1) production period, (2) capitalized interest, (3) eligible debt, (4) avoided cost debt, (5) advance payments, (6) property used in production, (7) calculation methods, (8) election requirements, and (9) partnership and S corporations.

Please evaluate current IRS regulations concerning interest-capitalization requirements for a small business in filing tax returns and prepare specific guidelines that can be successfully applied by Creative Plastics.

I'll look forward to receiving a draft of your report on or before November 1, 19--. Please let me know if you have any questions concerning this authorization.

Enc.

16.3. Transmittal Letter

[Letterhead]

November 16, 19--

Ms. Marilyn J. Sutter, Manager
Creative Plastics, Inc.
270 West End Avenue, N.E.
Washington, D.C. 20260

Dear Ms. Sutter:

INTEREST-CAPITALIZATION TAX GUIDE

I'm happy to enclose a copy of the report you requested on September 12 concerning tax-reporting guidelines on interest capitalization.

The report provides rules and guidelines concerning the treatment of capitalized interest on tax returns, including the calculation methods and election requirements. It also explains the accepted definition of qualified property and eligible debt.

I hope that the report will help you to determine the reporting requirements of Creative Plastics. Please let us know if we can be of any further help.

Sincerely,

Carl P. Darrell, CPA

Enc.

16.4. Table of Contents: Short Form

CONTENTS

16.5. Summary

SUMMARY

Under the uniform capitalization rules, you must
generally capitalize interest on debt that you use to
finance the production of real or tangible personal
property. This property must be used in your trade
or business or held for sale to customers.

The Internal Revenue Service treats capitalized
interest as a cost of the property produced. It is
recovered through the cost of goods sold, an
adjustment to basis, depreciation, amortization, or
another method. To determine the amount of interest
to be capitalized on qualified property, you must
first capitalize the interest on debt directly
allocable to the property's costs of production
(traced debt). The IRS allows any reasonable method
of calculation that you apply consistently.

Publications 538 and 551, appended to this
report, provide additional information on the
interest-capitalization rules.

v

16.6. Acknowledgments

ACKNOWLEDGMENTS

I want to thank the following persons who read a draft of this report and provided constructive comments: Natalie Scrocroft, CPA, managing partner, National Accounting Services; Vincent Truesdale, CPA, general manager, National Accounting Services; and Nora Rawson, IRS representative. I also want to thank the Department of the Treasury and the Small Business Administration for providing useful forms and publications.

16.7. Report Opening Page

1. Introduction

Under the uniform capitalization rules, you must generally capitalize interest on debt that is used to finance the production of real or tangible personal property.(1) The property must be used in your trade or business or held for sale to customers. Interest on a debt on property that was acquired and held for resale does not have to be capitalized.

This report will examine the Internal Revenue Service requirements pertaining to qualified property, the production period, capitalized interest, interest allocation method, traced debt, eligible debt, advance payments, property used in production, calculation methods, and election requirements.

The interest that you paid or incurred during the production period (see Glossary) must be capi-

---

Portions of this report were adapted from the Tax Guide for Small Business (Washington, D.C.: Department of the Treasury, Internal Revenue Service, 1992).

1

16.8. Report Closing Page

Interest Capitalization   24

12. Conclusions and Recommendations

The interest capitalization rules, described
above, are applied first at the level of the partnership or S corporation and then at the level of the
partners or shareholders to the extent that the
partnership or S corporation has insufficient debt to
support the production or construction expenses.(4)

If you are a shareholder in an S corporation,
you may have to capitalize interest you incur during
the tax year with respect to the production costs of
the S corporation. Similarly, you may have to
capitalize interest incurred by the S corporation
with respect to your own production costs. Refer to
IRS Notice 88-89, 1988-2 CB 422 (copies attached).
You must provide the required information in an
attachment to the Schedule K-1 to properly capitalize
interest for this purpose.

If you are a partner in a partnership, you may
have to capitalize interest you incur during the tax
year with respect to the production costs of the
partnership.(5) Similarly, you may have to capitalize
interest incurred by the partnership with respect to

16.9. Appendix Opening Page

<pre>
                        APPENDIX

Guide to Exclusions

A. Eligible Debt Exclusions

   1. Permanently nondeductible interest (such as

      tax-exempt interest)

   2. Personal interest (such as investment interest)

   3. Qualified home mortgage interest

   4. Interest incurred by a tax-exempt organization

      (unless directly connected to the organizatin's

      unrelated trade or business)

   5. Interest attributable to a debt between you and

      certain related parties (or between such

      parties themselves), if the rate of interest is

      less than the applicable federal interest rate

      on the date issued

B. Nondeductible Interest

   1. Interest on a debt incurred to buy or carry

      tax-exempt securities

   2. Amounts paid or incurred in connection with
</pre>

25

16.10. Appendix Closing Page

Appendix   26

$1,200,000 that is an eligible debt, bearing interest at a 10 percent annual rate.

1. Capitalize the interest incurred on the traced debt during the production period of the property.
2. Capitalize interest incurred on the avoided cost debt during that period, consisting of $600,000 of the $1,200,000 obligation, at a 10 percent annual interest rate.
3. Treat this $600,000 portion of that loan as avoided cost debt regardless of the particular financial or regulatory accounting treatment of the debt and regardless of the purpose for which, or when in time, you incurred the loan.

Interest Rate on Avoided Cost Debt

1. The interest rate on avoided cost debt is generally a weighted average of the interest rates on your eligible debt outstanding during the production period.
2. It does not include debt that has been specifically traced to the production activity.

16.11. References

NOTES

1. Jacob Clarney discussed this topic at length in his book <u>Interest Capitalization</u> (Washington, D.C.: Tax Consultants, 1991), 100-104, 201-2, 220-26.

2. Ibid.

3. For a case study of a firm similar in size and operation to Creative Plastics, see Mary Cromwell and Jerry Bransom, "Interest Capitalization: A Case Study," <u>Accounting Principles</u> 21, no. 4 (June 1990): 12-17.

4. Clarney, <u>Interest Capitalization</u>, 201.

5. Ibid.

6. Cromwell and Bransom, "Interest Capitalization," 15.

16.12. Glossary

GLOSSARY

Capitalized interest. A cost of the property produced that is recovered when the property is sold, used, or otherwise disposed of under the rules that apply to such transactions.

Eligible debt. Includes all of your debt except the exclusions listed in the appendix.

Production period. For real property, the period that begins when physical activity is first performed on the property.

Qualified property. Real property, personal property with a class life of twenty years or more, personal property with an estimated production period of more than two years, or personal property with an estimated production period of more than one year if the estimated cost of production is more than $1 million.

Traced debt. Eligible debt equal to or less than the qualified property's accumulated production costs and debt directly attributable to the production of qualified property.

28

WRITING PRESS RELEASES

Models 16.13 and 16.14 illustrate the proper format for the opening and closing pages for a press release (also called a news release). Note that a release is always double-spaced and that a large margin is left at the top of the first page. This space is used by the receiving editor for writing a headline. Also notice the designation at the bottom of the second page. The symbol -30- tells an editor that this is the end of the release.

Press Release

16.13. Press Release Opening Page

[Letterhead]

For further information:
Lynda Curt
703-642-7171, x 8190

FOR IMMEDIATE RELEASE

Alexandria, Virginia, September 16, 19--. The 21st Annual Information Technology Conference will be held from Monday, May 6, to Thursday, May 9, at the Washington, D.C., Convention Center. Advance tickets are available at $45 per person from the Association of Advanced Technology, 2131 Center Court Boulevard, Alexandria, Virginia 22306. Door tickets will be sold on a first-come, first-served basis for $55.

The conference will feature numerous sessions and exhibits on key areas of information technology, including personal computers (PCs) in business, local area networks (LANs), CD-ROM applications, desktop publishing technology, Windows-based products, and security strategies.

-MORE-

16.14. Press Release Closing Page

Technology Conference   2

The keynote address will be delivered at the
7 p.m. dinner on Tuesday by Edward McMillan,
president of Future Technologies, Inc. McMillan will
speak on the globalization of information technology
in the 1990s and its impact on U.S. industry.

Thirty-two sessions are scheduled during the
four-day conference, and tickets include attendance
at sixteen selected sessions and the keynote dinner.
The exhibit will be open throughout the conference to
all attendees. It will feature the latest
information-technology products of international
manufacturers. City tours and entertainment
arrangements will be provided to spouses and children
of attendees.

Part
IV

FORMS

17

Communications Forms

IF there were no forms in an office to facilitate the communications function, the staff might have to be doubled. The time spent in recording and transmitting messages and other information would be overwhelming, and the work load facing secretaries every day would be formidable. However, numerous forms designed for rapid, effective communication are available both as printed forms and as software.

Major word processing programs have features that enable you to create your own forms. Specialized forms software is also available. Some programs offer a collection of standard forms on diskette, already designed and ready for you to fill in with your own data. Even on predesigned forms, you can usually specify your own headings for columns. Other software is designed to help you fill in or finish predesigned forms. Some programs have both features.

Even when you have an electronic forms file, you may want to keep a forms notebook or file folder with a hard-copy sample of every form. Additional forms can be printed out or simply photocopied from your notebook or file folder.

Models 17.1 through 17.19 are illustrations of common forms used in a modern business office to facilitate the communications function, but they are intended only as examples that can be modified to suit your own needs. (For record-keeping forms, see chapter 18.) The forms in this chapter were created using Word Perfect 5.1.

17.1
Action Request Form

```
                        ACTION REQUEST


Date _____

From _____

To _____

( ) Please telephone _____.

( ) Please reply to the attached.

( ) Please prepare a reply for _____'s signature.

( ) Please furnish information re attached.

( ) Please reply to appropriate person to handle.

( ) Please discuss attached with _____.

( ) Please advise if we can handle.

( ) Please note and return.

( ) _____
```

17.2
Agreement

AGREEMENT

This agreement is made this _____ day of _____,
19__, by and between _____ (the
Company), and _____ (the Agent). The
parties hereto agree as follow:

The Agent shall provide to the Company the following
services:

1. _____

2. _____

at the following rate: _____.

The Agent agrees to keep and submit a weekly time record
and receipts for any materials or supplies purchased on behalf of the Company and shall receive from the Company weekly
compensation for approved time and costs as specified above.

This Agreement may be modified by written consent of
parties or may be canceled upon thirty (30) days' notice by
either party.

For _____[Company]_____

President _____ Secretary _____

For _____[Agent]_____

By _____

17.3
Announcement: Event

```
                        ANNOUNCEMENT


Date:  _____

From:  _____

To:  _____


This is to inform you that the following activity is planned.
Please make appropriate arrangements to attend.


Event:  _____

Date:  _____

Time:  _____

Place:  _____

For further information, contact:  _____

       _____
```

17.4
Ballot

BALLOT

[ORGANIZATION NAME]
Election of Directors
For the Term _____ - _____

Please check Yes or No in the space provided for each name.
Sign and return the ballot in the enclosed envelope.

Yes No   Yes No

[ ] [ ] _____(name)_____   [ ] [ ] _____(name)_____

[ ] [ ] _____(name)_____   [ ] [ ] _____(name)_____

[ ] [ ] _____(name)_____   [ ] [ ] _____(name)_____

I vote for the following persons in place of the above nomi-
nees for whom I have cast a negative vote:

_____   _____

_____   _____

_____   _____

Signature _____ Date _____

PLEASE RETURN YOUR BALLOT BY _____, 19__. THANK YOU.

17.5
Change of Address Form

CHANGE OF ADDRESS

Please complete (print or type) and forward to:

_____

NAME

_____
Last, first, middle initial

OLD ADDRESS

_____
No. & Street, Apt., Suite, POB, or RD No.

_____
City, State, Zip Code

NEW ADDRESS

_____
No. & Street, Apt., Suite, POB, or RD No.

_____
City, State, Zip Code

17.6
Collection Notice

```
              FORGET SOMETHING?????

   Yes, your payment is past due . . . won't you take a moment
to mail us your check now?

   Many thanks for your cooperation.


         Invoice _____ Date Due _____ $ _____


  TO:

                            [Company Name]

                            [Address]
```

17.7
Executive Reminder Note

Addressee: Date of Letter:

                              HOLD

Re:

17.8
Mail Routing Slip

FOR YOUR INFORMATION

Date: _____

From: _____

Please review and forward.

	NAMES	INITIALS	DATE
1.	_____	_____	_____
2.	_____	_____	_____
3.	_____	_____	_____
4.	_____	_____	_____
5.	_____	_____	_____
6.	_____	_____	_____
7.	_____	_____	_____
8.	_____	_____	_____
9.	_____	_____	_____
10.	_____	_____	_____
11.	_____	_____	_____
12.	_____	_____	_____

17.9
Message Form: Visitor

```
                    VISITOR MESSAGE

To: _____    Date:_____

Taken by: _____    Time: _____


Visitor: _____

Company: _____

_____

Phone: _____

Messsage: _____

_____

_____

_____

        ( ) please call           ( ) please write
```

17.10
Meeting Notice: Directors

```
                    MEETING NOTICE

                  BOARD OF DIRECTORS


To: _____

Meeting Date: _____    Time _____

Place: _____

       _____

Deadline for Submission of Agenda Items: _____

              [ORGANIZATION/ADDRESS/PHONE]
```

17.11
Meeting Notice: Employees

```
                        MEETING NOTICE


Date:  _____

To:    _____

From:  _____


     The next regular monthly staff meeting will be held on

_____ at _____ in room _____.

Please notify this office (ext. _____) if you are unable to

attend.

     Thank you.
```

17.12
Meeting Notice: Stockholders

[COMPANY LETTERHEAD]

NOTICE OF SPECIAL MEETING OF STOCKHOLDERS
TO BE HELD ON _____

A special meeting of the stockholders of _____,
a corporation in the state of _____, has been called
and will be held on _____ at _____ at
the registered office of the Company, _____
_____.

The meeting will be held for the following purposes.

1. _____
2. _____
3. _____

If you do not expect to attend, please fill in, date,
sign, and promptly return the enclosed postage-paid proxy.

By order of the Board of Directors.

_____
Secretary

[Place]

[Date]

17.13
Meeting Waiver of Notice

[LETTERHEAD]

We, the undersigned, duly elected directors of

_____, do hereby severally

waive notice of time, place, and purpose of the regular

_____ meeting of directors of said corporation

and consent that the meeting be held at the _____

_____ in the city of _____, state

of _____, on the _____ day of _____,

19__, at _____ o'clock in the _____ noon. We do

further consent to the transaction of any business that may

properly came before the meeting.

Dated _____, 19__ Signed: _____
                                 President and Director

                                 _____
                                 Vice President and Director

                                 _____
                                 Secretary and Director

                                 _____
                                 Treasurer and Director

                                 _____
                                 Director

                                 _____
                                 Director

                                 _____
                                 Director

17.14
Orders: Renewal Form

[COMPANY NAME]

[Address]

Yes, please continue my enrollment in _____
_____, with all rights and privileges to which
I am thereby entitled.

My check for $ _____ is enclosed.

( ) 1 year $ ___   ( ) 2 years $ ___   ( ) 3 years $ ___

Name: _____

Company: _____

Address: _____

City, State, Zip: _____

17.15
Orders: Requisition Form

REQUISITION

( ) Supplies/Stock   ( ) Forms   Date _____

( ) _____   No. _____

To _____   Deliver to _____

_____   _____

_____   _____

Qty	Cat. No.	Description	Unit Price	Total Price

Total

Charge to Dept. _____ Account No. _____

Reequisition by _____ Date Required _____

Remarks _____

Authorized by _____

17.16
Petition: Formal

```
                        PETITION
                        [Date]


    WHEREAS    _____

    _____

    WHEREAS    _____

    _____

    WHEREAS    _____

    _____

    WE, the undersigned _____ of _____

do hereby petition _____ to _____

    _____

    _____

    _____
```

Signature	Address	Date

17.17
Petition: Informal

PETITION FOR

_____

We, the undersigned, hereby request that _____

_____

_____.

SIGNATURE   ADDRESS   DATE

17.18
Proxy Form

PROXY

I hereby constitute _____, _____,

and _____ (who are officers or directors of the

company), or a majority of such of them as actually are

present, to act for me in my stead and as my proxy at the

_____ meeting of the stockholders of _____

_____, at _____, and at any adjourn-

ments thereof, with full power and authority to act for me

in my behalf, with all powers the I, the undersigned, would

possess if I were personally present.

Effective Date _____

Signed _____   _____
                Stockholder   City   State

17.19
Registration Confirmation Form

```
          REGISTRATION CONFIRMATION
          [Meeting Title, Place, Date]


M  _____

   _____

Your registration is confirmed for the following events:

Conference/Workshop Sessions:   ( ) Tuesday    ( ) Wednesday

Lunch:   ( ) Tuesday   ( ) Wednesday        Dinner: Tuesday

Received $ _____        Due on or before (date) $ _____

        [NAME OF SPONSORING ORGANIZATION/ADDRESS/PHONE]
```

18

Record-Keeping Forms

EFFICIENCY is a principal objective in the modern business office. Secretaries must constantly seek simpler and better ways to organize and control the massive amount of information that must be recorded and maintained every day. An indispensable tool in this task is the record-keeping form, which may be anything from a cross-reference sheet to a petty cash voucher.

Many record-keeping forms, like the communications forms described in chapter 17, can be purchased in office-supply stores as printed forms or created and filled in on your computer, using a word processing program that has this feature or a specialized forms-creator and forms-finisher program. You may find that the forms you design yourself are more suitable for your needs and easier to work with. Although you should store the forms in your computer file, you may also want to keep a folder or notebook of samples for desk reference and photocopying as duplicates are needed.

Models 18.1 through 18.51 are examples of useful record-keeping forms. The purpose of the forms is to provide a fast and easy means for organizing, recording, and maintaining information. Most of the models are intended only as samples; you should change them as necessary to fit your own work requirements. (See chapter 17 for examples of communications forms.)

18.1
Activity Record: Form

ACTIVITY RECORD [Name] [Period Covered]									
Date	**Time Spent per Activity**								**Total Hrs. per Day**
	A	B	C	D	E	F	G	H	
Mon,_____									
Tues,_____									
Wed,_____									
Thrs,_____									
Fri,_____									
Total hours per activity									

18.2
Activity Record: Long-Range Schedule

LONG-RANGE SCHEDULE

Project _____ Completion Date _____

Director _____ Telephone _____

Type of Activity	Summary of Activity	Dates and Times	Deadlines
Transportation			
Meetings			
Special assignments			
Miscellaneous			

18.3
Appointment Schedule: Daily

DAILY APPOINTMENT SCHEDULE [Date]		
Date	With Whom	Nature of Appointment

18.4
Appointment Schedule: Monthly

	APPOINTMENT SCHEDULE		
	[Month]		
For _____ Department _____			

Day	With Whom	Nature of Appointment	Comments
1			
2			
3			
4			
5			
6			
7			
8			
9			
10			
11			
12			
13			
14			
15			
16			
17			
18			
19			
20			
21			
22			
23			
24			
25			
26			
27			
28			
29			
30			
31			

18.5
Appointment Schedule: Travel

		TRAVEL APPOINTMENT SCHEDULE [Period] For _____ Department _____		
Date	Time	With Whom (Address)	Telephone	Comments

18.6
Appointment Schedule: Weekly

WEEKLY APPOINTMENT SCHEDULE

[Week of _____ to _____]

Date	Time	With Whom	Nature of Appointment
Mon,_____			
Tue,_____			
Wed,_____			
Thrs,____			
Fri,_____			

18.7
Balance Sheet: Form

CURRENT BALANCE SHEET

[Company]

as of [Date]

ASSETS   LIABILITIES

Current   Current
Assets   Liabilities

Cash $_____   Accounts
                                                 payable $_____
Accounts
  receivable   _____   Accrued
                                                 expenses   _____
Inventory   _____
                                               Short-term
                                                 loans   _____

Fixed Assets   Fixed
                                               Liabilities

Land $_____   Long-term
                                                 loan $_____
Building $_____
                                               Mortgage   _____
Equipment   _____

  Total   _____
                                               Net Worth $_____
Less

  Deprec.   _____ $_____

                                               Total
Total assets $_____   Liabilities $_____

18.8
Budget: Form

CASH BUDGET

For Quarter Ending _____

Item	[Month]		[Month]		[Month]	
	Budget	Actual	Budget	Actual	Budget	Actual
EXPECTED CASH RECEIPTS:						
1. Cash sales						
2. Collections on accounts receivable						
3. Other income						
4. Total cash receipts						
EXPECTED CASH PAYMENTS						
5. Raw materials						
6. Payroll						
7. Other factory expenses (including maintenance)						
8. Advertising						

[Continued on next page]

18.8
Budget: Form

9. Selling expense	
10. Administrative expense (including salary of owner-manager)	
11. New plant and equipment	
12. Other payments (taxes, including estimated income tax; repayment of loans; interest; etc.)	
13. Total cash payments	
14. Expected cash balance at beginning of the month	
15. Cash increase or decrease (item 4 minus item 15)	
16. Expected cash balance at end of month (item 14 plus item 15)	
17. Desired working cash balance	
18. Short-term loans needed (item 17 minus item 16, if item 17 is larger)	
19. Cash available for dividends, capital cash expenditures, and/or short investments (item 16 minus item 17, if item 16 larger than item 17)	
CAPITAL CASH:	
20. Cash available (item 19 after deducting dividends, etc.)	
21. Desired capital cash (item 11, new plant equipment)	
22. Long-term loans needed (item 21 less item 20, if item 21 is larger than item 20)	

18.9
Cash Forecast: Estimate Form

CASH FORECAST

[Year]

Item	Jan	Feb	Mar	Apr	May	Jun	Jul	Aug	Sep	Oct	Nov	Dec
1. Cash in bank (start of month)												
2. Petty cash (start of month)												
3. Total cash (add 1 and 2)												
4. Expected accounts receivable												
5. Other money expected												
6. Total receipts (add 4 and 5)												
7. Total cash and receipts (add 3 and 6)												
8. All disbursements (for month)												
9. Cash balance at end of month in bank account and petty cash (subtract 8 from 7)												

18.10
Charge-Out Slip

```
                    CHARGE-OUT SLIP

                       [Department]


Date Removed:_____    Return Date:_____

Subject:_____

Description of Material:_____


_____

_____

Name:_____    Telephone:_____

Department:_____
```

18.11
Collection Notice: Card Follow-up Record

```
                      COLLECTION FOLLOW-UP


Name: _____    Account No.: _____

Address:_____    Ref. No.: _____


Type of Account: _____

Amount Due: _____

Terms: _____

Due Date(s): _____

Past-Due Amount/Date: _____


Collection Action: _____

_____

                                  Date: _____
```

18.12
Committee-Membership List

COMMITTEE-MEMBER LIST [Committee Name/Organization]		
Name/Address/Phone	Term of Service	Special Assignments

18.13
Conference Planning Form

Duties	Contact (Person, Organization)	Deadline for Arrangements	Date Completed
CONFERENCE PLANNING FORM [Meeting Title, Date]			
1.			
2.			
3.			
4.			
5.			
6.			
7.			
8.			
9.			
10.			
11.			
12.			

18.14
Contributions Record

	CONTRIBUTIONS, 19___ [Name]	
Date	Organization	Amount

18.15
Corrective Action Plan: Form

CORRECTIVE ACTION PLAN				
Problem			Date	
			Work Units	
Workstation/ Resp. Worker	Operations	Start Date	Completion Date	Follow-up Date
Confirm Permanent Correction (Action/Date/By)		Remarks		

18.16
Credit-Card Record

CREDIT CARD RECORD [Name]			
Date Card Issued or Account Opened	Expiration Date	Issuing Company	Card or Account No.

18.17
Cross-Reference Sheet

CROSS-REFERENCE SHEET

Name/Subject: File No.:

Re: Date:

SEE

Name/Subject: File No.:

18.18

Dividends Income Record

Stock/Bond	Shares	J	F	M	A	M	J	J	A	S	O	N	D	Annual Total
Monthly Total														

DIVIDEND RECORD, 19___

18.19

Facilities Checklist: Meeting

<table>
<tr><td colspan="6">FACILITIES CHECKLIST

[Meeting Title, Time, Place, Date]</td></tr>
<tr><th>Item</th><th>Room</th><th>Equipment
Needed</th><th>Special
Requirements
(or Problems)</th><th>Deadline for
Arrangements</th><th>Date
Completed</th></tr>
<tr><td>1.</td><td></td><td></td><td></td><td></td><td></td></tr>
<tr><td>2.</td><td></td><td></td><td></td><td></td><td></td></tr>
<tr><td>3.</td><td></td><td></td><td></td><td></td><td></td></tr>
<tr><td>4.</td><td></td><td></td><td></td><td></td><td></td></tr>
<tr><td>5.</td><td></td><td></td><td></td><td></td><td></td></tr>
<tr><td>6.</td><td></td><td></td><td></td><td></td><td></td></tr>
<tr><td>7.</td><td></td><td></td><td></td><td></td><td></td></tr>
<tr><td>8.</td><td></td><td></td><td></td><td></td><td></td></tr>
<tr><td>9.</td><td></td><td></td><td></td><td></td><td></td></tr>
<tr><td>10.</td><td></td><td></td><td></td><td></td><td></td></tr>
<tr><td>11.</td><td></td><td></td><td></td><td></td><td></td></tr>
<tr><td>12.</td><td></td><td></td><td></td><td></td><td></td></tr>
</table>

18.20
Follow-up Note

```
                    FOLLOW-UP RECORD

                     [Department]


Due Date:  _____

Re:  _____

Submit to:  _____

Requested by:  _____

Action Taken:  _____

_____

          Date:  _____  By:  _____
```

18.21
Gift Record

GIFTS, 19___ [Name]					
To Whom Given	Gift Given	Occasion	Cost	Other Suggestions	Suggested Price

18.22
Income Statement: Form

INCOME STATEMENT

Year Ended _____

Gross sales $ _____

Cost of sales:

  Opening inventory $ _____

  Purchases   _____

    Total   _____

  Ending inventory   _____

    Total cost of sales   _____

Gross income   _____

Operating expenses:

  Payroll (employee)   _____

  Rent   _____

  Payroll taxes   _____

  Interest   _____

  Depreciation   _____

  Truck expense   _____

  Telephone   _____

  Insurance   _____

  Miscellaneous   _____

    Total   _____

Net income (before owner salary) $ _____

18.23

Insurance Records: Life

LIFE INSURANCE

[Name of Insured]

Type of Policy	Company	Date of Issue	Beneficiary	Amt.	Annual Prem-ium	Disability		Double Indem-nity	Premium Due Dates
						Prem. Waiver	Monthly Income		

18.24

Insurance Records: Policies

INSURANCE POLICIES

[Name of Insured]

Type of Insurance	Company	Policy No.	Agent	Premium	Period Covered	Due Dates	Dates Paid	Check No.

18.25
Insurance Records: Property

PROPERTY INSURANCE

[Name of Insured]

Type of Policy	Company	Policy No.	Agent	Kind of Prop.	Loca-tion	Prem-ium	Period Covered	Dates Due	Dates Paid	Check No.

18.26
Insurance Records: Premiums

```
                    INSURANCE PREMIUMS


Company: _____   Policy No.:_____

Type of Policy: _____   Coverage: _____


Insured: _____

Agent: _____


Premium: _____   Expiration Date: _____

Due Dates: _____


Pay to: _____

_____
```

18.27
Interest Income Record

INTEREST INCOME

[Owner's Name]

[Period]

Taxable Income			Tax-Exempt Income		
Description	Date Received	Amount Received	Description	Date Received	Amount Received
Total $			Total $		

18.28
Investments: Current

CURRENT INVESTMENTS [Name of Investor]					
Type of Security	Name of Security	No. of Shares & Face Val.	Cost of Security	Current Market Price	Date of Maturity
Stocks					
Bonds					
Mutual funds					
Investment totals					

18.29
Investments: Transactions

INVESTMENT TRANSACTIONS [Name of Investor]		
Transaction Information	Purchases	Sales
Registered name		
Certificate no.		
Date of purchase/sale		
No. of shares		
Kind of security		
Price per share		
Total sales/purchase price		
Commission		
Misc. charges (e.g., taxes)	N/A	
Short-term capital gain (loss)	N/A	
Long-term capital gain (loss)	N/A	

18.30

Mail: Correspondence Digest

		CORRESPONDENCE DIGEST		
		[Date]		
Date of Corresp.	From	Summary of Message	Action Required	Action Taken

18.31
Mail: Summary Record

		MAIL SUMMARY			
Date Rec'd	From	Subject	To Whom Sent	Action Required	Follow-up Date

18.32
Medical Expenses Record

			Amount Paid	
			Medicine & Drugs	Other Expenses
Date	Description of Expenses	To Whom Paid		

MEDICAL EXPENSES, 19____

[Name]

18.33
Meeting Dates Record

MEETING DATES RECORD

[Period Covered]

Type of Meeting	Scheduled Dates											
	Jan	Feb	Mar	Apr	May	Jun	Jul	Aug	Sep	Oct	Nov	Dec

18.34
Merit Rating Chart

MERIT RATING [Date/Employee]			
Performance Factor	Above Average	Average	Below Average
Personality			
Cooperation			
Dispostion			
Neatness			
Leadership ability			
Initiative			
Industriousness			
Judgment			
Accuracy			
Quality of work			
Quantity of work			
_____			
_____			
_____			
_____			
_____			
_____			
_____			
_____			
_____			

18.35
Minutes: Recording Form

```
                          MINUTES
                          [Date]


Meeting Date _____    Place _____


Present:


    _____    _____

    _____    _____

    _____    _____


Call to Order:


Reading, Correction, and Approval of
Minutes of Previous Meeting:


Correspondence:


Reports of Officers:


Reports of Standing Committees:


Reports of Special Committees:


Unfinished Business:


New Business:


Appointment of Committees:


Nominations and Elections:


Announcements:


Adjournment:

                                    _____
                                    Secretary
```

18.36
Minutes: Resolution

RESOLUTION

Adopted _____

WHEREAS _____

_____

WHEREAS _____

_____

WHEREAS _____

_____

RESOLVED, That _____

_____

_____

FURTHER RESOLVED, That _____

_____

_____

_____   _____
Secretary   Chair

18.37
Petty Cash Record

		PETTY CASH RECORD [Department]		
Date	Voucher Number	Explanation	Receipts	Payments

18.38
Petty Cash Voucher

PETTY CASH VOUCHER

[Department]

Date: _____   No.: _____

Charge to Account: _____   Amount: _____

Paid to: _____

For: _____

Approved by: _____

Received: _____

18.39
Receipt: Document

```
                        DOCUMENTS RECEIPT

                         [Department]
─────────────────────────────────────────────────────────────

Date Removed: _____   Due Date: _____

Released to: _____

_____   Telephone: _____

For: _____

Description of Document: _____

_____

                        Approved: _____
```

18.40
Receipt: General

```
                                              No. _____

[COMPANY NAME]

  [Address]

                                         Date _____


Received from _____

The Sum of _____ Dollars $ _____

For _____ ( ) cash ( ) check ( ) M.O.


Amount of Account      $ _____
                                           THANK YOU!
Amount Paid            $ _____

Balance Due            $ _____


                                         By _____
```

18.41
Records Retention Form

RECORDS RENTENTION		
[Department]		
Description of Record	Period to Be Retained	Special Requirements
1.		
2.		
3.		
4.		
5.		
6.		
7.		
8.		
9.		
10.		
11.		
13.		
14.		
15.		
16.		
17.		
18.		
19.		
20.		

18.42

Supplies: Control Record

INVENTORY-CONTROL RECORD

[Department]

Item	Average Qty Used/ Month	Number on Hand											
		1/31	2/28	3/31	4/30	5/31	6/30	7/31	8/31	9/30	10/31	11/30	12/31

18.43
Supplies: Inventory Record

		SUPPLIES-INVENTORY RECORD [Department]		
Date	Quantity	Item	Purpose	Price

18.44
Tabulation Form: Scheduled Events

SCHEDULED EVENTS								
[Scheduled Dates]								
Event #1 Date _____			Event #2 Date _____			Event #3 Date _____		
Yes	No	Maybe	Yes	No	Maybe	Yes	No	Maybe

18.45
Telephone: Long-Distance Calls Record

LONG-DISTANCE CALLS

Telephone Number: _____

To: _____

_____

Re: _____

_____

Placed by: _____ Date: _____

Time: _____ Charges: _____

18.46
Time-Work Analysis Form

	TIME-WORK ANALYSIS [Date]				
Job	Morning		Afternoon		Total Minutes
	Start	Finish	Start	Finish	
A					
B					
C					
D					
E					

18.47

Travel: Authorization

TRAVEL AUTHORIZATION

Name _____ Date _____

Department _____ Tavel Order No. _____

From/To	Dates	Purpose	Types of Transp.	Transp. Cost	Living Expense	Enter- tainment	Mics.	Total Cost

Total Travel Advance $ _____ cash $ _____ check

_____
Approved

_____
Date

18.48

Travel: Expense Report

EXPENSE REPORT

Name _____   Period Covered _____

Title _____   Department _____

Date	Transportation			Living Expense		Enter-tainment	Phone Fax Postage	Misc.	Daily Total
	Auto	Plane	Train	Hotel	Meals				
Total									

Item	Current Month	Previous Month	Year to Date
Mileage			
Expenses			
Budget			

18.49
Travel: Itinerary

ITINERARY: [NAME]

[Period]

From	To	Flight (Train)	Departure Date/Time	Arrival Date/Time	Travel Accom.	Car Rental Arrangement	Hotel Accom.	Reminder

18.50
Travel: Itinerary Worksheet

INTINERARY WORKSHEET

Name _____ Period Covered _____

DATE

Lv: _____ Time _____ Plane/Train _____ Accom. _____

Ar: _____ Time _____ Airport/Sta. _____ Car Rental _____

Hotel _____ Address _____

Appointments:

Reminders:

18.51
Travel: Supplies Checklist

TRAVEL-SUPPLIES CHECKLIST

[ ] Letter stationary

[ ] Memo stationary

[ ] Envelopes, plain

[ ] Envelopes, addressed
     to company

[ ] Large mailing envelopes

[ ] Legal/letter pads

[ ] Postage stamps

[ ] Address book/list

[ ] File folders

[ ] Business cards

[ ] Mailing schedule

[ ] Calendar

[ ] Mailing boxes or folders
     for dictation and
     computer disks, tapes, etc.

[ ] Dictation equipment

[ ] Dictation belts, tapes
     disks, etc.

[ ] Computer equipment

[ ] Computer diskettes, tapes, etc.

[ ] Expense forms

[ ] Other forms

[ ] Files

[ ] Cash

[ ] Personal checkbook

[ ] Credit cards

[ ] Business checkbook

[ ] Business credit cards

[ ] Travel guides and maps

[ ] Catalogs, brochures, etc.

[ ] Itinerary

[ ] Appointment schedule

[ ] Timetables and flight
     schedules

[ ] Reservation confirmation

[ ] Tickets

[ ] Passports, visas, etc.

[ ] First aid kit

[ ] Pens, pencils, erasers

[ ] Paper clips

[ ] Scissors

[ ] Rubber bands

[ ] Stamp pad and rubber stamp

[ ] Cellophane tape

[ ] Pins

[ ] Bottle opener

[ ] Ruler

Part

V

LETTER-WRITING AIDS

19

Letter and Memo Formats

THE first impression of a letter or memo is created by the way it looks—its general appearance, including neatness, accuracy, and format. Most readers will glance next at the inside address and salutation to see if their names are spelled correctly. Since first impressions are so important, it is clear that an acceptable format and a correct name and address are essential to the effectiveness of the message. In fact, all of the technical aspects are important in creating the desired impression (see chapter 20 for instructions concerning the proper use of the principal elements in letters and memos). To maintain a consistent appearance and to save formatting time later, store the models in your computer for later recall.

FORMATTING YOUR MESSAGES

Letters are prepared in one of five common formats: full block (19.1), block (19.2), modified block (19.3), simplified (19.4), and of-ficial/personal (19.5). (See model 19.6 for an example of the format for a continuation page.)

Which format you should use depends on the requirements of your employer. Your office may have a preferred layout; otherwise, you should select a layout appropriate for the image your company wants to convey. A conservative or traditional format, such as the modified-block layout, would be suitable for a bank, whereas a more casual, modern look, such as the simplified format, would be appropriate for a modern novelty manufacturer. Ease of setup may be a consideration in some offices, particularly those using typewriters rather than computers. The block and simplified formats, for example, do not require indenting or centering keystrokes. If you are in doubt, ask your boss for his or her preference.

Memos can be prepared in a number of ways. The standard format (19.7) is often used on regular business letterhead or standard size memo letterhead. Some printed memo forms, available in office-supply stores, use a message-reply format (19.8). A note format (19.9) can be used for very brief handwritten or typed notes prepared on small note-size paper. When a memo runs over to additional pages, the standard format should be used, with a continuation-page heading (19.10) similar to that used for letters.

Envelopes for external mailings are prepared in one of two formats: the traditional style (19.11) or the modern OCR style (19.12). The OCR style is required by the U.S. Postal Service when the mail is to be sorted using optical character reading equipment. Depending on the postal station where mail is deposited, use of the OCR style can mean faster processing and delivery.

For larger packages, businesses may use printed mailing labels from office-supply stores, or they may have their own labels designed and printed. Model 19.13 illustrates a basic mailing address format, and model 19.14 illustrates a combined address and data format.

See models 19.15 through 19.17 for examples of three common business-card formats: managerial (19.15), chief executive (19.16), and professional (19.17). Printers have numerous examples of styles suitable for all types of businesses and positions, in standard black and white or in color.

Setting Up Letters

19.1. Full-Block Format

[Letterhead]

January 4, 19--

Your reference 612Z-92

Ms. Janet Grove
Bellweather Industries, Inc.
1121 Baker Lane
Princeton, N.J. 08540

Attention Belinda Shoupe

Dear Ms. Grove:

FULL-BLOCK FORMAT

This is an example of the full-block letter format.
This format is popular in organizations seeking an
efficient and modern letter form.

No indentions are used in this style. Everything is
set flush left, which saves time and energy in
formatting.

Because the name of the person dictating is given in
the signature, his or her initials are not included in
the identification line.

Sincerely yours,

Alan Carson, Jr.
Correspondence Secretary

md

Enc. 1

P.S. For computer-formatting instructions, follow the
requirements of your word processing software. AC

19.2. Block Format

[Letterhead]

January 4, 19--

Your reference 612Z-92

Ms. Janet Grove
Bellweather Industries, Inc.
1121 Baker Lane
Princeton, NJ 08540

Attention Belinda Shoupe

Dear Ms. Grove:

BLOCK FORMAT

Some businesses use a variation of a blocked letter
style. Like the full-block format, the block letter
also saves time and energy.

The inside address and paragraphs are positioned flush
left. However, the dateline and reference line are set
slightly right of the page center. The complimentary
close is also positioned slightly to the right of the
center of the page, with the signature aligned beneath
it.

Since the name of the person dictating is given in the
signature, his or her initials are not included in the
identification line.

Sincerely yours,

Alan Carson, Jr.
Correspondence Secretary

md

Enc. 1

P.S. For computer-formatting instructions, follow the
requirements of your word processing software. AC

19.3. Modified-Block Format

[Letterhead]

January 4, 19--

Your reference 612Z-92

Ms. Janet Grove
Bellweather Industries, Inc.
1121 Baker Lane
Princeton, N.J. 08540

Attention Belinda Shoupe

Dear Ms. Grove:

MODIFIED-BLOCK FORMAT

The modified-block format is preferred in those companies that want to present a traditional image. It does not, however, have all of the timesaving setup features of the full-block and block styles.

The paragraphs, as well as the subject line and postscript, are indented one-half to one inch, but in all other respects it resembles the block format. The dateline, reference line, and complimentary close, for example, begin slightly to the right of the page center.

Because the name of the person dictating is given in the signature, his or her initials are not included in the identification line.

Sincerely yours,

Alan Carson, Jr.
Correspondence Secretary

md

Enc. 1

P.S. For computer-formatting instructions, follow the requirements of your word processing software. AC

19.4. Simplified Format

[Letterhead]

January 4, 19--

Your reference 612Z-92

Ms. Janet Grove
Bellweather Industries, Inc.
Princeton, N.J. 08540

Attention Belinda Shoupe

SIMPLIFIED FORMAT

The simplified format, Ms. Grove, is a modern version
of the full-block letter. Like the full-block format,
everything is positioned flush left.

This format differs from all others in that it omits
the salutation and complimentary close. Instead, the
writer mentions the recipient's name at the beginning
and end of the letter body. Also, an extra line space
is added where the salutation and complimentary close
were omitted.

Because the name of the person dictating is given in
the signature line, Ms. Grove, his or her initials are
not included in the identification line.

Alan Carson, Jr.
Correspondence Secretary

md

Enc. 1

P.S. For computer-formatting instructions, follow the
requirements of your word processing software. AC

19.5. Official/Personal Format

[Letterhead]

January 4, 19--

Dear Ms. Grove:

The official format is often used in personal correspondence on executive-size (or monarch) stationery. The principal difference in this format from the others is the placement of the inside address. Also, it usually does not have all of the parts of a regular business letter, such as the subject line or reference line.

The salutation is placed about five or six line spaces below the dateline. Paragraphs are indented, and the dateline, complimentary close, and signature are positioned slightly right of the page center. The inside address is placed two line spaces below the last signature line, flush left.

An identification line is usually not included on the original copy of an official/personal letter.

Sincerely yours,

Alan Carson, Jr.
Correspondence Secretary

Ms. Janet Grove
Bellweather Industries, Inc.
1121 Baker Lane
Princeton, N.J. 08540

19.6. Continuation Page

[COMPANY NAME, STREET, CITY, STATE, ZIP CODE]

Janet Grove
January 4, 19--
page two

and the continued page of a letter should observe the
same style as the first page in regard to indentions
and position of elements.

Sincerely yours,

Alan Carson, Jr.
Correspondence Secretary

md

Enc. 1

P.S. For computer-formatting instructions, follow the
requirements of your word processing software. AC

Setting Up Memos

19.7. Standard Format

[Letterhead]

TO: Janet Grove   **DATE:**   April 4, 19--

FROM: Alan Carson, Jr.   **REF. NO.:** 612Z-92

SUBJECT: STANDARD MEMO FORMAT

FOR: ( ) **Action**   ( ) **Decision**   (X) **Information**

Here's a model of the standard memo format. As you can see, the preliminary information is provided by way of guide words (TO, FROM, and so on).

Most memos are set up in a flush-left format, with no paragraph indentions. Although there is no complimentary close or signature line in the standard format, notations such as Enc. are positioned flush left the same as in a letter.

If you have any other questions, Ms. Grove, please let me know. I appreciate your interest.

md

Enc. 1

P.S. For computer-formatting instructions, follow the requirements of your word processing software. AC

19.8. Message-Reply Format

[Letterhead]

TO: Janet Grove   **DATE:** January 4, 19--
Bellweather Industries
1121 Baker Lane   **REF. NO.:** 612Z-92
Princeton, N.J. 08540

SUBJECT: MESSAGE-REPLY MEMO FORMAT

MESSAGE

    Here is a model of the message-reply memo format, Ms. Grove. Notice that the key feature of this type of memo is that it has a place for the recipient to reply on the same form. Often this style has two or three carbon or carbonless parts so that both the sender and receiver can retain one copy for their files.

                 Signed *Alan Carson, Jr.*

REPLY

Signed_____ **Date**_____

19.9. Note Format

M E M O

From Alan Carson, Jr.

This is an example of the small note
format, Ms. Grove. It is used when the
sender just wants to make a brief comment.
Usually, the sender's name is printed at the
top, as illustrated above.

19.10. Continuation Page

[COMPANY NAME, STREET, CITY, STATE, ZIP CODE]

Janet Grove
January 4, 19--
page two

and the continuation page of a standard memo is very
similar to that of a letter, except that the complimentary close and signature lines are omitted as they
are on all memos.

md

Enc. 1

P.S. For computer-formatting instructions, follow the
requirements of your word processing software. AC

Preparing Envelopes

19.11. Traditional Format

BROCK OFFICE SERVICES
1000 Newton Boulevard
Oakland, CA 94610   *[postage]*

Confidential   REGISTERED

                        Ms. Janet Grove
                        Bellweather Industries, Inc.
                        1121 Baker Lane
                        Princeton, N.J. 08540

19.12. OCR Format

BROCK OFFICE SERVICES
1000 Newton Boulevard
Oakland, CA 94610   *[postage]*

RETURN POSTAGE GUARANTEED   SPECIAL DELIVERY

[begin 2"   JANET GROVE
from bottom   BELLWEATHER INDUSTRIES INC
of envelope]   ATTN BELINDA SHOUPE
                     1121 BAKER LANE   RM 601
                     PRINCETON NJ 08540-1234

            [at least 1"left & right margins,
                5/8" bottom margin]

Preparing Mailing Envelopes

19.13. Mailing Address Format

BROCK OFFICE SERVICES
1000 Newton Boulevard
Oakland, CA 94610

TO: Janet Grove
Bellweather Industries, Inc.
1121 Baker Lane
Princeton, NJ 08540

FIRST CLASS

19.14. Mailing Address-Data Format

BROCK OFFICE SERVICES
1000 Newton Boulevard
Oakland, CA 94610

(X) **First Class**	**RETURN POSTAGE GUARANTEED**
( ) **Priority**	
( ) **Third Class**	
( ) _____	**TO:** Janet Grove
( ) _____	Bellweather Industries, Inc.
( ) _____	1121 Baker Lane
( ) _____	Princeton, NJ 08540
( ) _____	

Formatting Business Cards

19.15. Managerial

```
601-497-5613                    601-497-5614


              WALTON KITCHEN AIDS
           Accessories for the Modern Kitchen


      Juliet Peterson       1673 Abernathy Road
      Sales Manager         Montgomery, AL 36117
```

19.16. Chief Executive

```
              JONATHAN FINCHLEY III
                  President

           Finchley, Hill & Hood
              Kennedy Court
             2102 Brettina Lane
              Boston, MA 02165
               617-321-3295
```

19.17. Professional

```
   For  ___Tanya Veneto_____
   Date _March 7, 19--__ at __3__ o'clock


              ARLENE PROTTLE, D.D.S.
               Telephone 301-9087


   12 Butler Street      Annapolis, MD 21401
```

20

Principal Elements of Letters

and Memos

LETTERS and memos have many elements that must be written and positioned properly on a page so that the message will appear professional and create a favorable impression. Common letter and memo formats were illustrated in chapter 19; here, the principal parts of those letter and memo formats are described in the order in which they appear on the page.

TECHNICAL ASPECTS OF A BUSINESS MESSAGE

A business letter may contain more than a dozen elements such as the reference line (20.2), the salutation (20.6), and the complimentary close (20.11). Your office probably follows a certain practice in the use and placement of these technical aspects of correspondence. For example, perhaps you use an identification line (20.13) only on the copies but never on the original. Aside from such requirements, you should write and position the various elements according to the format your office prefers (see chapter 19).

Models 20.1 through 20.18 describe the principal elements of a business letter, and models 20.19 through 20.24 describe the principal elements of a memo. Included among these sections are descriptions of effective letter openings (20.9) and closings (20.10), correct forms of address (20.6), and the proper heading for a continuation page (20.18 and 20.24). The formats in chapter 19 for traditional and OCR envelopes (19.11-19.12) illustrate the proper placement of the elements of an envelope used for outgoing mail. In-house memos are commonly sent by company messenger in an unsealed, reusable routing envelope, with ruled lines on the outside where names of recipients can be written and then crossed off after the person has removed his or her mail.

Setting Up the Principal Parts of Letters

20.1. Dateline

Write the date two to four line spaces below the letterhead address. Place it flush left in the full-block and simplified formats and slightly right of the page center in the other formats. In a business letter, the proper order is month, day, and year; in military style, the order is day, month, and year, with no commas.

> *Business:* January 1, 19--

> *Military:* 1 January 19--

20.2. Reference Line

Write the reference line two line spaces below the dateline and align it on the left with the dateline. If a printed line, such as "In reply please refer to" appears on the letterhead, write the reference code or number after the printed line, which is usually above the date. If you have two designations (Our reference, Your reference), place your own reference code or number first.

> January 1, 19--
>
> Your reference ABC-0101

> When replying, refer to: ABC-0101
>
> January 1-19--

> January 1, 19--
>
> Our reference ABC-0101
> Your reference ABC-0101

20.3. *Personal or Confidential Notation*

Use a personal or confidential notation if you don't want anyone but the addressee to open the letter. Always place this notation flush left regardless of the format. Position it about four line spaces above the inside address or two line spaces below the reference line. It may be all capitals or with initial capitals only and underlined.

PERSONAL

Personal

CONFIDENTIAL

Confidential

20.4. *Inside Address*

Write the inside address single-spaced in uppercase and lowercase letters even if the envelope address is in all capitals (OCR style). Place it flush left in all formats, usually two to twelve line spaces below the date or reference line. In the official/personal style, place it two line spaces below the signature.

Follow these rules for spelling: (1) Spell the addressee's name exactly as he or she writes it. (2) Use the company's official name. (3) Spell out street numbers of twelve and below (131 North Twelfth Street). (4) Use figures for all house numbers except *One* (2 Fifth Avenue). (5) Use a spaced hyphen between house and thoroughfare numbers (239 - 18 Street). (6) Abbreviate city names only if that is the preferred spelling (St. Paul). (7) Use the person's business title only if it won't cause an address to run over four lines, and place a short title on the same line as the person's name (Ms. Danielle Adams, Manager). (8) List the departmental name on a separate line beneath the company name. (9) Stack the names of two or more persons by importance of title, if any, or otherwise alphabetically.

Mr. Jacob Schoenberg, President
Ms. Anne Laurel, Manager
Michael's Electronic Systems
3000 Western Shores
Pullman, WA 99164

See 20.6 for correct forms of address for men, women, companies, professional people, and dignitaries.

20.5. *Attention Line*

Use an attention line when you want a letter addressed to a company to be directed to a specific person. Also, use it when you want a letter addressed to an individual to be opened by another person if the addressee is absent. Place an attention line flush left in all formats except the official/personal, where it should not be used. Leave one line space before and after it in most formats, with two line spaces after it in the simplified format. Add a title or department if the person works in a large company.

Attention Lois Kingman, Business Office

Attention Barry Clark, Managing Director

20.6. *Salutation*

Position the salutation, or greeting, flush left in all letter formats except the simplified style, which has no salutation. Place it two line spaces below the inside address or attention line (if any) in all formats except the official/personal style, where it appears two to twelve line spaces below the date.

Use the opening word *Dear* in business letters followed by the person's name or by the title when the name is unknown. Precede the person's last name with a personal or scholastic title such as *Ms.* or *Dr.*, but not with an occupational title such as *treasurer* or *programmer.*

Close friend or associate:	Dear Jerry:
Untitled Man:	Dear Mr. Marx:
Titled Man:	Dear Dr. Marx:
Untitled Woman:	Dear Ms. Jones: (*Mrs.* if she prefers)
Titled Woman:	Dear Dr. Jones:
Single Untitled Man and Woman:	Dear Mr. Fox and Ms. Steele: (*Mrs.* if she prefers)
Married Untitled Man and Woman (business):	Dear Mr. Fox and Ms. Fox: (*Mrs.* if she prefers)

Married Untitled Man and Woman (formal social):	Dear Mr. and Mrs. Fox:
Married Titled Man and Untitled Woman (business):	Dear Dr. Fox and Ms. Fox: (*Mrs.* if she prefers)
Married Titled Man and Untitled Woman (formal social):	Dear Dr. and Mrs. Fox:
Married Untitled Man and Titled Woman (business):	Dear Dr. Fox and Mr. Fox:
Married Untitled Man and Titled Woman (formal social):	Dear Dr. and Mr. Fox:
Married Titled Man and Titled Woman (business):	Dear Drs. Fox:
Married Titled Man and Titled Woman (formal social):	Dear Drs. Fox:
Two Men:	Dear Mr. Pulaski and Mr. Ortega: (or Dear *Messrs.* Pulaski and Ortega)
Two Women:	Dear Ms. Stryker and Ms. Polerno: (or *Mrs.* if either prefers)
Firm of Men:	Gentlemen: (or *Messrs.*)
Firm of Women:	Ladies: (or *Mesdames*)
Firm of Men and Women:	Ladies and Gentlemen:
Collective:	Dear Friends: (or *Members* etc.)
Name Unknown but Title Known:	Dear Director: (or *Editor* etc.)

Gender Unknown but Name Known:	Dear A. M. Hartshorne:
Name Unknown but Gender Known:	Dear Sir: (or Madam)
Title, Name, and Gender All Unknown:	Dear Sir or Madam:
Professional-Business Person but No Academic Degree:	Dear Ms. Clarke:
Professor, Dean, etc. but No Academic Degree:	Dear Professor/Dean Stowe:
Dignitaries (informal):	Dear Mr. President:
	Dear Mr. Chief Justice:
	Dear Ms. Secretary: (cabinet)
	Dear Senator Hill:
	Dear Mr. Chairman/Dear Senator Hill: (committee)
	Dear Mr. Ambassador/Dear Ambassador Hill:
	Dear Captain Hill:
	Dear Cardinal Hill:
	Dear Reverend Father Hill:
Dignitaries (formal):	Mr. President:
	Sir: (chief justice)
	Madam: (cabinet)
	Sir: (senator)
	Dear Mr. Chairman: (committee)
	Madam: (ambassador)
	Dear Captain Hill:
	Your Eminence: (cardinal)
	Dear Reverend Father Hill:

See also the discussion of the inside address (20.4).

20.7. Subject Line

Place the subject line two line spaces below the salutation in general business letters (above in legal letters). The word *subject*, if used, is often written in all capitals followed by a colon. (Lawyers use *In re.*) Indent the subject line when a format with paragraph indentions is used (modified block and official/personal); otherwise position it flush left. It may be in all capitals or with initial capitalization of important words. Underlining may be used if desired.

SPRING EXHIBITION STATUS REPORT

Spring Exhibition Status Report

SUBJECT: SPRING EXHIBITION STATUS REPORT

SUBJECT: Spring Exhibition Status Report

Spring Exhibition Status Report

20.8. Body

Start the body, or message, two line spaces below the salutation or the subject line (if any). Single-space the body and leave one line space between paragraphs (a brief, one- or two-sentence message may be double-spaced). Use margins of one to two inches depending on the length of the letter. Indent paragraphs one-half to one inch in the modified-block and official/personal formats; begin paragraphs in the other formats flush left. Lists or long quotes should be indented on the left and, if desired, on the right the same as each paragraph indent or an additional amount. When a letter runs over to a second page (see 19.10 in chapter 19), carry at least two lines of the body over to the continuation page. For guidelines on a continuation-page heading, see 20.18.

20.9. Effective Openings

To capture a reader's attention, make your opening lines short and get straight to the point. Use natural language and avoid dull, stilted phrases. Mention the person's name if it will sound natural. When news is involved, use an approach summarizing who, what, when, where, why, and how. Other techniques for effective openings include the use of a question, an interesting or unusual fact, a quotation, or a reference to a famous person.

Thank you, Bill, for reminding me about the September deadline for my committee report.

I was so pleased to read about your appointment in this morning's newspaper.

Have you ever wondered what would happen to your electronic equipment if our city should experience a serious power outage?

20.10. Effective Closings

Use endings that will leave the reader with the impression you want to make or that will motivate the person to take the action you want. Avoid dull, stilted endings and outmoded language. Have a positive attitude and use positive words. Don't conclude by asking the reader to do several things--offer only one alternative; also, when appropriate, mention a specific deadline for any action you request.

> We have a copy of our free booklet waiting for you; all you need do is check the box on the enclosed postage-paid card and mail it today.

> Please call me at 445-0911 by Monday, September 16, if you can join me, Louise. I'm looking forward to seeing you again.

> Ms. Perry, your suggestion will be invaluable to our reorganization plan, and we all greatly appreciate your important contribution.

20.11. Complimentary Close

Place the complimentary close two line spaces below the body, flush left in the full-block and simplified formats and slightly right of the page center in the other formats. Capitalize only the first word and place a comma after the last word. Use a formal closing in letters to dignitaries and other people of very high rank, but use an informal close in most ordinary business letters, particularly if you know the person well.

Informal: Sincerely,
Sincerely yours,
Cordially,
Cordially yours,
Regards,
Best regards,
Warmest regards,
Best wishes,

Formal: Very sincerely yours,
Very cordially yours,
Very truly yours,
Yours very truly,
Yours truly,
Respectfully,
Respectfully yours,

20.12. Signature

Place the signature line four line spaces below and aligned with the complimentary close (20.11) in all formats except the simplified style, where it is placed five lines below the body since there is no complimentary close in that format. If a job title is included, place a short title after the person's name and a long title on the line below the name. Use the full official names of companies, and write a person's name *exactly* as he or she signs it (with or without initials and so on).

Do not precede the name with a title such as *Mr.* or *Ms.* unless the gender is not otherwise clear. Use *Miss* or *Mrs.* only if the signer wants to be addressed that way. Women should use their preferred last name—maiden, married, or a combination. In strict formal social usage, a married or widowed woman places the words *Mrs.* and her husband's full name all in parentheses (*Mrs. Walter Royal*) but signs with her first name and married last name: *Anna Royal*. A divorced woman may use *Mrs.* with her maiden name and former married last name combined (*Mrs. Jenkins-Somerset*) but signs with her first name and the last name: *Kathryn Jenkins-Somerset*. Secretaries often sign their employer's name on routine letters or when the employer is absent or busy. If you do this, sign the name as it is typed in the signature line and put your initials directly underneath the signed name. If you type your name in the signature line and sign the letter, the correct title is: *Secretary to Mr./Ms. Conners* (omit your employer's first name).

Single woman:

Dana Parks
Dana Parks

Dana Parks
(Miss) Dana Parks

Married or
widowed woman:

Dana Parks
Dana Parks

Dana Parks
(Mrs.) Dana Parks

(Mrs.) Dana Jarvis-Parks

(Mrs. James Parks)

Divorced woman:

Dana Parks

Dana Jarvis

(Miss) Dana Jarvis

(Mrs. Jarvis-Parks)

(Mrs.) Dana J. Parks

Dana Jarvis-Parks

Man:

Arnold Kilmer, Jr.

Gender unknown:

(Ms.) D. J. Parks

(Mr.) A. O. Kilmer

Title or degrees
included:

Dana Parks

Dana Parks, M.D.

Arnold Kilmer, Jr.

Arnold Kilmer, Jr.
Director of Product Testing

Firm name included: Sincerely,

Kilmer Accounting Services

Arnold Kilmer, Jr.

Arnold Kilmer, Jr., CPA
General Manager

20.13. Identification Line

Write the initials of an identification line, if one is used, flush left two line spaces below the signature lines on all formats. However, initials are usually not used with official/personal letters. Some firms omit this line on the original and include it only on the file copy. If the letter writer (or dictator), signer, and preparer consist of three different people, use three sets of initials. Omit the writer's initials if his or her name appears in the signature line. Place a colon between each set of initials, with no space around the colon.

RGC:dn

RGC:SJ:dn

dn

20.14. Enclosure Notation

In all formats except the official/personal style, place the enclosure notation flush left two line spaces below the identification line. If the letter is very long, single-space around the various notations and identification line. In the official/personal style, place the enclosure notation flush left two line spaces below the inside address.

Enc.

1 Enc.

Encs.

Encs. 3

Encs.: Contract
Address List

Enclosures

20.15. Mail Notation

Place the mail notation flush left two line spaces below the enclosure notation in all formats. Single-space in a very long letter if all other notations are single-spaced.

Certified

Registered

By United Parcel Service

By messenger

20.16. Copy Notation

Place the copy notation flush left two line spaces below the mail notation in all formats (it is generally not used in an official/personal letter). The abbreviation *pc* (photocopy) is occasionally used in place of *c* or *Copy*. Single-space in a very long letter if all other notations are single-spaced. A blind-copy notation (*bc*) means that no one else but the blind-copy recipient knows it has been sent. Place the blind notations only on the recipient's copy and the file copy.

c: Robert Sharpe

Copy: Robert Sharpe

Copies: Robert Sharpe
Cynthia Bonsall

pc: Robert Sharpe

bc: Jane Watts

20.17. Postscript

Place the postscript(s) two line spaces below the last notation line, flush left in the full-block and simplified formats and with a paragraph indent in the other formats. A postscript should convey something generally unrelated to the body of the letter. It should not consist of something that a writer forgot to include in the body that is being added as a postscript because the writer is too sloppy or lazy to redo the letter properly. If a writer has two postscripts, use *P.P.S.* for the second (post-postscript). Place the writer's initials (without periods) one or two character spaces after the last word of the postscript.

> P.S. I'll call you next week about rescheduling the committee meeting. ACF

> P.P.S. Is it true that our supplier may close its control warehouse? ACF

20.18. Continuation-Page Heading

Place the continuation-page heading three to four line spaces after the printed continuation-page name and address. If you have no continuation-page stationery, use a blank sheet that matches the letterhead and begin four to six lines from the top. Do not use the word *continued* at either the end of the first page or top of the second page. Write the heading--addressee's name, date, and page number--in one of the standard layouts illustrated below: (1) each item stacked below the other; (2) in a single line flush left with commas between each item; or (3) centered across the entire page with no commas between items. The addressee's personal or scholastic title may be used or omitted, as desired. (See also 19.10 in chapter 19.)

> Ms. Edna Harvey
> December 14, 19--
> page two

> Edna Harvey, December 14, 19--, page 2

> Ms. Edna Harvey   December 14, 19--   page 2

Setting Up the Principal Parts of Memos

20.19. Guide Headings

If the stationery you use for memos does not have guide words (*To, From,* and so on) printed on it, add those words with your typewriter or computer in a standard layout such as those shown below (see also the memo formats in chapter 19). Businesses differ in the amount of information they want to include in the headings and in the position of guide words. Even brief memos, however, usually include the date, to, from, and subject. Capitalize and punctuate the subject and other guides, such as the reference number, the same as you would do in a letter. See 20.1, 20.2, 20.5, and 20.7.

```
DATE:        November 5, 19--
TO:          Roland Schroeder
FROM:        Liz Hochner
SUBJECT:     Auto-Stop Sorter
```

```
TO:        Roland Schroeder          DATE:     November 5, 19--
           Service Department
                                     REF. NO:  OYJT-1191
FROM:      Liz Hochner
           Mail Room

SUBJECT:   Auto-Stop Sorter
```

```
DATE:      November 5, 19--              REF.:   OYJT-1191
TO:        Roland Schroeder          FROM:  Liz Hochner
           Service Department Mail Room        Mail Room
SUBJECT:   Auto-Stop Sorter
```

20.20. Body

Begin the body of a memo three to four line spaces below the guide words. Use margins of one to two inches depending on the size of the memo. Write the body single-spaced with or without paragraph indents. Double-space between paragraphs. (Some standard forms available in office-supply stores have ruled lines for the body as well as printed guide words.) Follow the same style for writing subheads, lists, blocked quotations, and other elements as you would use in a letter. (See examples throughout this book, particularly in chapters 13 and 16.) Generally, leave one to two spaces above and below a blocked quotation and the items in a list. Also, leave one to two spaces above and below any subheadings in report memos.

20.21. Identification Line

Place the identification line flush left two to four line spaces below the last line of the memo body. Memos usually are not signed, so there is no complimentary close or signature line. Some writers, however, sign their initials two line spaces below the last line of the body, slightly right of the page center. If that is done, place the identification line two line spaces below those initials. Follow the same rules concerning the placement of the writer's, signer's, and preparer's initials as in a letter (20.13).

DKF:MR:sl

20.22. Notations

The same notations used in a letter are used in a memo: first the enclosure notation (20.14), next the mail notation (20.15), and then the copy notation (20.16). Stack these notations below the identification line flush left, double-spaced or, in a very long memo, single-spaced. Refer to 20.14-20.16 for guidelines on how to capitalize, abbreviate, and punctuate the various notations.

stc

Enc. 3

By Federal Express

c: Elton Johnston
Avis Pennyworth

20.23. Postscript

Write the postscript two line spaces below the last notation line, flush left or indented the same as the body's paragraph style. Use *P.P.S.* for a second postscript, as illustrated in 20.17. Like letter postscripts, the memo *P.S.* should consist of an additional thought generally unrelated to the text of the memo. But it should not consist of something the writer simply forgot to put in the body. After the last word, type the sender's initials (without periods).

P.S. I've ordered some posters to spruce up the lobby and will call you when they arrive. FB

20.24. *Continuation-Page Heading*

Memos that run to a second page are generally prepared on standard-size business letterhead or memo paper of the same size. Matching blank sheets can be used if printed second sheets are unavailable. Place the continuation heading at the top of the second page three to four line spaces below a printed address line (if any); otherwise, begin four to six lines from the top of a blank sheet. Write the heading—addressee's name, date, and page number—in one of the basic layouts illustrated for letters (20.18). The person's title may be used or omitted, as desired. Many firms prefer the stacked version for its ease of setup.

Dr. Nancy Weatherby
April 17, 19--
page three

Index